More
POINTS SCHMOINTS!

By Marty Bergen

Magnus Books

Magnus Books
34 Slice Drive
Stamford, Connecticut 06907-1133

First Edition published 1999.
Printed in the United States of America.
10 9 8 7 6 5 4 3 2 1

First Printing: October, 1999

Library of Congress Catalog Card Number
99-75213

ISBN 0-9637533-5-5

Dedication

To my wonderful wife, Cheryl
All my love forever

CONTENTS

ACKNOWLEDGMENTS

Thanks To:

Eleanor Bengyak, Nancy and Earl Conway, Harry Falk, John Hardy, Tannah Hirsch, Spike Lay, Ellen Pomer, Nancy Sahlein, Bob Sawyer, Alan and Dorothy Truscott and Steve Weinstein.

My Very Special Thanks To:

Nancy Deal, Dennis Daley, Nancy DeWeese, Jim Kaplan, Susan Katz, Mary Oshlag and Ginny and Jeff Schuett.

The Stars

I cannot say enough to thank Larry Cohen, Patty Magnus and Richard Oshlag for all that they did to make this sequel a success. Take that and magnify it a hundred times and you will get an idea of the gratitude I owe Cheryl Bergen, my helper, my wife and my friend.

INTRODUCTION
The Making of a Sequel

DATELINE October, 1996 — The Editor Cracks the Whip

Riiinnnnnggggggg. "Hello, Marty speaking but can you call back?"

"Impatient editor speaking. No, I can't. *Points Schmoints!* is doing great...but it's time for the sequel, Marty. Stop loafing around and get to work. I want four articles by next week."

"Patty, are you nuts? Game four of the World Series is going on. I can't talk now. The Yankees are rallying after trailing by six runs. Call me next year."

"Marty, we can't wait. Tape the silly game, watch it tomorrow! We need..."

Sound of TV "It is high, it is far, it is gone. That home run ties it up. The Yankees have come alllllll the way back!"

"Yesssss. See ya, Patty." Bangggg as Marty's phone is slammed down.

October 1997 — If at First You Don't Succeed

Riiiinnnnnnnng. "Who can be calling at 1:30 in the morning? MARTY, answer the phone." Wife Cheryl is not pleased.

"Hello, Marty speaking but asleep."

"Patty speaking. Next year is here! Your time is up, write me something! What are you waiting for? Dennis told me that your damn Yankees are not in the World Series this year. You have no excuse. I'll settle for three..."

"Patty, your timing is still bad. It's football season. The Jets have Parcells now and we're hot. No guy does any work from September until after the Super Bowl. You should know that. Hasn't Dennis taught you anything?"

Loud crasshhhh as the receiver of Patty's phone goes flying into the wall.

July 1998 — No More Mr. Nice Guy (Gal)

"Marty, there is no football now (I checked) and the Yankees are way ahead (Dennis said so). There is no sports you need to watch. Get moving."

"Good news and bad news, Patty. We ARE moving... to Florida in the fall. By the way, I'm too busy packing to even think about writing."

"MARRRRRTYYYYYYYYYY. It's been FOUR years."

"No hurry. After we arrive, we'll need to unpack, then I'll be busy teaching. Call me in the 21st century, let's see, "2001, A Bridge Odyssey. Not bad.""

"That's it, I've had it. You are HOPELESS! Unless you promise to have this book in print before the end of this century, I'm going to call you every single day...until you crack. And you will! You think I'm kidding? Ask Dennis..."

"No, that's okay. I give up. I'll do ANYTHING to avoid YOUR daily reminders. You win. I promise to have the book done on time. Don't call me, I'll call you." Two phones are hung up.

"Let's see. I still have plenty of time. When does Wimbledon go on? Where's my remote? Cherylll?

March 1999 — A Wake-Up Call

"Dennis, wasn't that a great final four? College basketball is the best."

"Sure is, Marty. How's the sequel going? Patty talks about you all the time. Sometimes the words she uses even have more than four letters!"

"SEEQUELLLL? Gotta Go, Dennis, thanks." Both hang up phones. "Think, Marty, think, where's my computer?" CHERYLLL?

August 1999 — My Kingdom for a Title (A Reader Comes to the Rescue)

"Dear Marty. I love your book, but I've reread it 11 times, I know it cold. The Rule of 20, page one. Mrs. Bennett shoots her husband, page 35. Rule of 11, Chapter 11 (cute, Marty). What is scary is that I'm spouting all this with the book closed. My friends and I are bored. We need more points schmoints."

"Yeeessssssss."

Five Minutes Later

Rinnnnnnnnngggggggggggg. "Marty? Marty who?"

"Cute. Okay, you're entitled. I just had a brainstorm. Simple but says it all. We'll call our new book *More Points Schmoints*!"

Now, with time to spare, we proudly present our sequel. Enjoy.

CHAPTER 1
Points Schmoints! Revisited

Mastering *Points Schmoints!*

Many serious readers of *Points Schmoints!* have told me that they have reread that book several times, and proceeded to challenge me to test them. Your wish is my command. I have carefully structured the following to give those of you who have not read that book a fighting chance.

Assume that neither side is vulnerable for each of the following (the page numbers refer to *Points Schmoints!*).

For the first three problems, choose your call after dealing.

♠ 86
♡ AQ73
◇ 6
♣ KJ10762

Open 1♣. Your hand meets the requirements of The Rule of 20—ten HCP plus ten cards in your two longest suits (pp. 1-4).

♠ 6
♡ 763
◇ K86
♣ KJ10942

Open 3♣. Because an opening 2♣ bid shows a strong hand, it is sometimes necessary to open 3♣ with a good six-card suit (p. 82).

♠ AQ
♡ J43
◇ Q765
♣ KQ103

Open 1♣. I will never understand why players believe that they must open all hands that have four diamonds and four clubs with 1◇ (p. 8).

On the next two deals, the auction proceeds as follows, with the opponents silent:

Partner	You
1♡	1♠
2♣	???

♠ K743
♡ 52
◇ AJ1084
♣ 104

Bid 2♡, taking a preference. **A preference is no stronger than a pass**, it merely states that you are in a playable spot. If you really liked hearts, you would have indicated that at your first turn (p. 31).

♠ AQ742
♡ A5
◇ 973
♣ K86

Bid 2◇, fourth-suit forcing to game. This bid says nothing about diamonds and leaves the next move to partner (pp. 25-27).

For the next three hands, you are East and the auction proceeds:

West	North	East	South
1♠	Dbl	???	

What would you do?

♠ Q832
♡ 76
◇ 94
♣ 109865

Jump to 3♠. This weak jump raise is supported by The Law of Total Tricks (The LAW)—with nine trumps you are happy to compete to the three level (p. 64).

♠ 9
♡ Q753
◇ K94
♣ AQJ53

Redouble, showing at least ten points. The opponents may already be out of their depth, and you hope to teach them a sharp lesson. A 2♣ bid would show a weak hand (pp. 61-63).

♠ A1097
♡ AQ5
◇ 9753
♣ 109

Bid 2NT, Jordan. This excellent convention allows responder to show both strength and support directly after the opponent's takeout double (p. 66).

Your partner opens 1NT and RHO passes. Now what?

♠ 74
♡ 85
◇ K92
♣ AQJ753

Bid 3NT. Do not worry about the majors; partner is a solid favorite to have them stopped. 5♣ is very unlikely to be the best contract (pp. 15-16).

♠ J765
♡ 9864
◇ Q1063
♣ 5

Respond 2♣, Garbage Stayman. You plan to pass opener's rebid, confident that you will do better playing in two of a suit than in 1NT (pp. 13-14).

Partner opens 1♡ and your RHO overcalls 1NT. What is your call?

♠ 984
♡ 7
◇ KQJ743
♣ 987

Bid 2◇. This bid does not require strength, only a nice suit (pp. 72-74).

Remember, partner opens 1♥ and RHO overcalls 1NT.

♠ K10
♥ K9
◇ A8765
♣ 9753

Double for penalty. This is the only way to show strength after an opponent overcalls 1NT (pp 72-74).

This time your RHO opens 1◇. What action would you take?

♠ 4
♥ A9863
◇ AK7
♣ AK98

Bid 1♥. Do not make takeout doubles when short in an unbid major, even with a big hand (pp. 50-52).

♠ K76
♥ AQ7
◇ 53
♣ A8743

Double—much more flexible than a two-level overcall on a lousy suit (pp. 67-71).

♠ AQJ6
♥ 96
◇ AQ9
♣ 9853

Overcall 1♠. A very strong four-card suit is perfectly acceptable for a one-level overcall (p. 71).

Your LHO opens 1♣, which is passed around to you. Now what?

♠ KQ4
♡ AJ7
◇ 9762
♣ KQJ

Double. In the balancing seat, a 1NT bid would show less than a 1NT opener. You will bid notrump after partner's response, promising 15-18 HCP (pp. 75-80).

♠ AKJ1074
♡ KJ4
◇ 75
♣ 63

Jump to 2♠. In balancing seat, the jump overcall is not preemptive (pp. 75-80).

You are South for the last two "problems" and the auction proceeds:

West	North	East	South
1♡	2♠	3♠	???

♠ K4
♡ 842
◇ 98753
♣ A84

Double East's artificial 3♠ bid, asking partner to lead spades. Without the double, you would not expect him to lead away from his ♠AQ10732 (pp. 183-185).

♠ K764
♡ 76
◇ A9873
♣ 76

Bid 4♠ with your ten-card fit, following The LAW. If doubled, you expect to lose less than the opponents would have scored in 4♡ (pp. 21-24).

I hope you enjoyed this review of *Points Schmoints!* Now, on to more of a good thing.

The Return of The Rule of 20

What topic in *Points Schmoints!* drew the most attention—and more importantly—the most acclaim? I had predicted that **The Battle of the Sexes** would garner the lion's share, but it was not even close. The runaway winner was **The Rule of 20**.

I would like to believe that all bridge players read *Points Schmoints!* Sadly enough, however, there are some who never did (I will consider forgiving their oversight, especially since it is not too late). Therefore, allow me to take a moment to review this excellent guideline.

Question: When should The Rule of 20 be applied?

Answer: When you are considering whether your hand is strong enough to open 1♣, 1♢, 1♡ or 1♠ in first or second seat.

Question: How should this rule be used?

Answer: Add the length of your two longest suits to your HCP. When the total is 20 or more, open the bidding.

Question: What about majors versus minors, and vulnerability?

Answer: Not to worry. Here are some examples. Several are taken directly from *Points Schmoints!* (with the author's permission, of course).

♠ KQ54	12 HCP
♡ A873	4 spades
♢ 6	4 hearts
♣ K1064	_____
	20 — Open 1♣.

♠ AQJ865	10 HCP
♡ —	6 spades
♢ 972	4 clubs
♣ K754	_____
	20 — Open 1♠.

♠ KJ975	10 HCP
♡ Q8	5 spades
◊ A965	4 diamonds
♣ 64	
	19 — Pass.

♠ 87	11 HCP
♡ Q76	7 diamonds
◊ AKQ9765	3 hearts
♣ 5	
	21 — Open 1◊.

What was the key to the popularity of **The Rule of 20**? Answer: it was so easy. Whatever your bridge level, applying The Rule of 20 required nothing more than arithmetic. Of course, that would not count for much if it were not accurate, but it is. Using it does not guarantee that you will always make your contract, or that you will get a good result on every hand. However, in the long run, you will do very well.

As alert readers pointed out, blindly following The Rule of 20 can lead to certain illogical conclusions. For example:

♠ K
♡ QJ
◊ Q5432
♣ Q5432

Technically, this hand fulfills The Rule of 20. Of course, opening it is a total joke.

♠ AQ1098
♡ A1098
◊ 1098
♣ 10

This hand only totals 19. I will state for the record that no amount of persuasion would result in my passing with these promising cards.

I was aware of all this when I explained The Rule of 20 in *Points Schmoints!* Why did I deliberately omit these hands and keep things simple? I hoped that *Points Schmoints!* would transcend level and appeal to all players—inexperienced as well as experienced, social as well as duplicate. My feedback suggests that I attained this goal—everyone seemed to relate well to The Rule of 20.

The time to "tell all" is here. Allow me to set you straight on the finer points of The Rule of 20—to give you the graduate version of the undergraduate work done in *Points Schmoints!*

However, if you like the status quo, do not be concerned. I am not going to present anything radical or complicated. If you are happy with The Rule of 20 as you know it, you can take the following with a grain of salt or even ignore it. What I propose to do is refinement, not major surgery.

Rule of 20 Refinements—"Subtractions"

Subtract one point for each of the following short-suit honor combinations:

Singleton king, queen or jack (all but the ace).

Subtract one point for these dubious doubletons:

King-queen; king-jack; queen-jack (again, note that the ace is not involved).

Rule of 20 Refinements—"Additions"

Add one point for the following:

Two tens, especially when they are in combination with higher honors in suits that are three or more cards in length.

Rule of 20 Refinements
Rating Honor Cards

Aces and kings are underrated, be prepared to **upgrade**.

Queens and jacks are overrated—hands with a lot of these cards should be **downgraded**.

When in doubt, open!

As I said earlier, do not allow your new knowledge to complicate your life. Bridge is difficult enough, without my adding to it. I always want readers to enjoy The Rule of 20 for its simplicity and accuracy.

Okay, enough chatter from me. Here are some examples you can use to practice The Rule of 20.

♠ A1085	10 HCP
♡ A72	5 diamonds
♢ Q10954	4 spades
♣ 4	<u>+1 for the two tens</u>
	20 — Open 1♢. This is my kind of hand.

♠ QJ	12 HCP
♡ K6543	5 hearts
♢ KJ6	3 diamonds
♣ Q87	<u>- 1 for the doubleton QJ</u>
	19 — Pass. Ugly.

♠ Q432	12 HCP
♡ QJ65	4 spades
♢ QJ7	4 hearts
♣ A4	<u>- 1 for too many queens and jacks</u>
	19 — Pass.

♠ A953	12 HCP
♡ 952	4 spades
♢ A63	3 hearts
♣ A84	<u>+1 for the aces</u>
	20 — Open 1♣. Always open with three aces.

♠ K742	12 HCP
♡ K	4 spades
◇ QJ93	4 diamonds
♣ QJ82	<u>- 1 for the singleton king</u>
	19 — Pass.

♠ 64	9 HCP
♡ AJ10854	6 hearts
◇ A1086	4 diamonds
♣ 3	<u>+1 for the helpful tens</u>
	20 — Open 1♡, not 2♡.

I love this hand. It has great offense and adequate defense. Too many people open 2♡ and cannot figure out what went wrong when they miss a game. Would your partner consider inviting to game after you opened 2♡ and he held either of the following hands?

♠ A953 ♡ K7 ◇ KJ52 ♣ J62

♠ AK92 ♡ 97 ◇ K9 ♣ 98752

Obviously not.

There, that was not too painful. I hope that you did not mind our excursion to graduate school. Speaking for myself and my 2.14 GPA, I only wish that my college's curriculum had included more courses such as **The Rule of 20** rather than **Philosophy 101**.

Arlene Counts 'Em Up

While teaching in Long Island, NY, one of my favorite students was Arlene, a lovely lady who marched to her own drummer. One day, Arlene dealt herself the following hand and went into the tank before opening 1♢. Eventually, she became the dummy in a 4♠ contract. Everyone was staring at me when she tabled her hand:

♠ K1098   ♡ 2   ♢ AQ1098   ♣ 976

The disappointed declarer could not control herself. "What are you doing, Arlene? What a lousy hand! How could you open with only nine HCP?"

I searched for the perfect words to maintain peace. But I need not have worried. Arlene had the situation well in hand.

"Marty taught us that just as jacks are half as good as queens, tens are half the value of jacks. Two tens can be counted as one point. That brought me to ten. It follows that nines are half as good as tens—a quarter of a point each: I was now up to ten and three-quarters. Two eights equal one nine, and that one-quarter brings the total to 11. Add the five-card suit and the four-card suit, and this hand should be opened because it fulfills The Rule of 20!"

For the first and only time in our nine years together, the five other young ladies sat in stunned silence as they anxiously turned to me, awaiting my knowledgeable rebuttal.

I know that I have devoted thousands of hours to this wonderful game in the 37 years since I first opened a copy of *Five Weeks to Winning Bridge*. I firmly believe that I appreciate the value of spot cards as much as any player. However, I can honestly say that using eights as a criterion for opening was a new one on me. You certainly had to admit that Arlene's numeric skills were beyond reproach.

"Well done, Arlene. I cannot speak for others, but I have no problem opening a hand with such lovely texture."

By the way, 4♠ made easily.

Do Experts Apply The Rule of 20?

Only sometimes. How do they fare when they rely on their expert judgment to solve subsequent dilemmas? Sometimes well, but other times not so well. Here are two examples from top-level tournament play in 1999.

A world champion from the Women's Team Trials held this hand as dealer with both sides vulnerable. She passed, which seems very wrong to me. Not only does this hand satisfy The Rule of 20, but those lovely tens bring the total to 21. I will also remind readers of the power of six-four distribution.

Our Heroine	North	East	South
P!	1◇	P	1♠
2♣	2♠	3♣	4♠
5♣	P	P	Dbl
all pass			

Do I agree with the eventual 5♣ bid? No. One of my theories is that **many players, even experts, sacrifice too often in five of a minor**. As The LAW indicates, unless you have 11 trumps or once-in-a-lifetime distribution, **on most hands, the five level belongs to the opponents**.

Why did our heroine bid 5♣? She realized how good her hand was, especially once a fit had been established. I doubt that she expected to make 5♣ after partner's modest single raise, but she hoped to lose less than the opponents would score in 4♠.

How did she do? She went down two doubled, for a loss of 500 points. That would have been less expensive than 4♠ making, a duplicate score of 620. Unfortunately, the opponents had no chance to make 4♠. Her decision to bid on was therefore quite expensive.

What happened when the opposing team played this deal? The sensible player who held these cards opened 1♣ and was subsequently able to rebid that suit. Once she had given her partner a good description of her hand, she no longer had to guess at a high level.

I hope that you got the message. Regardless of your experience and ability, speaking as soon as possible is invariably more successful and makes this game easier than passing and guessing.

My second example is taken from the semifinals of the Spingold Master Knockout Teams, the premier event of the Summer Nationals. This time, the perpetrator was in second position following an opponent's pass. Only the opponents were vulnerable. If you admired West's distribution in our first example, this one will knock your socks off:

♠ —
♡ 6
♢ KJ109652
♣ AJ1097

Twelve cards in two suits—I have not held too many of those. The Rule of 20 resolves all doubts: nine HCP plus seven diamonds plus five clubs plus one (for the two relevant tens) totals 22, so I would have opened 1♢.

This hand was played at four tables and I would like to focus on the two auctions where the experts attempted to describe this hand with an initial pass! Were they able to catch up? You be the judge. Here are their auctions:

West	North	East	South
—	—	—	P
P!	1♢	1♠	2♡
3♣	3♡	P	4♡
all pass			

If you believe that West's one sign of life did justice to the cards he held, "you ain't seen nothing yet". Take a gander at the auction produced by the world champion at another table.

West	North	East	South
—	—	—	P
P!	1♢	1♠	2♡
P!!	3♡	P	4♡
P!!!	all pass		

Wow! This expert sat there and passed throughout. This spectacular display of nonbidding is exactly what he would have done holding:

♠ 432   ♡ 432   ♢ 5432   ♣ 432

Maybe I am crazy, but treating his hand in the identical manner as the Yarborough above leaves me speechless.

How did it work out? About as well as it deserved—4♡ was laydown for 11 tricks, a score of 650. Meanwhile, 5♢ doubled would be down only one for a loss of 100. What a surprise! The hand with seven-five distribution played better on offense than defense.

Do experts and world champions have great confidence in their ability to figure out what to do at any given moment? I will answer by saying that they do not suffer from a lack of ego. On most hands, they do just fine. There is no way that the average player can even hope to emulate that success. However, those players who appreciate The Rule of 20 can enjoy triumphs that are sometimes missed by the pass-and-guess contingent.

*   *   *

Speaking of bridge experts...

After a Charity Pro-Am bridge function, two experts were going over the boards from their game that evening. It is fair to say that neither Bob nor George had been impressed by their respective partners. In fact, they were arguing over which novice was worse.

"Let me tell you how my partner played 4♠ on board ten!" said Bob. He had the ♡64 in his hand and the ♡AQ in dummy. Would you believe, he crossed to dummy with a trump and led the ♡Q from the board? Fortunately for us, the finesse was offside and it didn't matter. I will bet you a pastrami sandwich that you can't top that."

"You're on," replied George. "On that same hand, the opponents made 4♠ against us. When the novice declarer made the same idiotic play of leading dummy's queen, my partner muttered 'second hand low' and ducked his king!!! By the way, I'll take mine lean with plenty of mustard."

CHAPTER 2
Sizing up the Hand

The Truth About Honors

Aces and kings are underrated. Queens and jacks are overrated. Those players who complain about "aces and spaces" are wrong, wrong, wrong. Compare the following two hands:

If you like pictures, go to a museum. If you prefer to win, take the hand on the left.

Honors in long suits are more valuable than those in short suits.

The first hand is far superior. Your chances of developing tricks in long suits are greatly enhanced when they include strength.

Before we proceed, it is worth mentioning that your opponents' bidding will affect the value of your honor cards. You prefer to have them sitting behind any honors the opponents have. For example, if RHO opens 1♡, your ♡K is worth more than if your LHO opens 1♡.

Honors in partner's long suit(s) are worth their weight in gold.

After the following auction, choose your action with each hand.

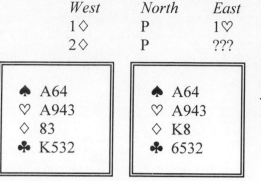

West	North	East	South
1◇	P	1♡	P
2◇	P	???	

♠ A64
♡ A943
◇ 83
♣ K532

♠ A64
♡ A943
◇ K8
♣ 6532

Bid 2NT with the first hand, but jump to 3NT confidently with the second one. The value of your ◇K is off the charts. Making game should be no problem.

Honor cards are enhanced when they are in combination with other honors. This is especially true for queens and jacks. The first hand below, therefore, is much better than the second:

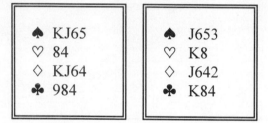

♠ KJ65
♡ 84
◇ KJ64
♣ 984

♠ J653
♡ K8
◇ J642
♣ K84

The concept of proven values is useful here. Honors which are proven are very likely to be helpful to partner. *Prime cards* (aces and kings) are assumed to be proven. Honors in partner's suit(s) are considered proven. Minor honors (stray queens and jacks) are considered unproven unless partner has promised length in their suit. The more proven values you have, the better your hand. For example, the auction proceeds:

West	North	East	South
1♡	P	2♡	P
3♣*	P	???	

* 3♣ is a game try.

You hold:

♠ Q72	♠ A54
♡ 643	♡ Q76
◇ Q863	◇ 8643
♣ A75	♣ Q92

With the first hand, you have only one proven value, the ♣A. You should sign off in 3♡. With the second, you are happy to jump to 4♡ because each of your three honors is "proven."

Cards like nines and tens can make a dramatic difference, especially when partner has not shown support. Take a look at the hands below.

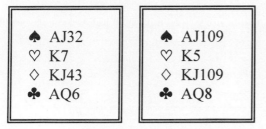

♠ AJ32	♠ AJ109
♡ K7	♡ K5
◇ KJ43	◇ KJ109
♣ AQ6	♣ AQ8

You do not believe that the first hand is as good as the second, do you? Look at those gorgeous spot cards. My goodness, in the world according to Arlene, the second hand is worth an extra one and a half points! I agree.

Evaluate the next two hands based on this auction:

West	North	East	South
1♠	P	1NT	P
???			

♠ AJ632	♠ AJ1097
♡ AQ743	♡ AQ1096
◇ A5	◇ A4
♣ 6	♣ 6

A 2♡ bid is sufficient with the first. You cannot afford to jump shift. Bid 3♡ with the second hand and force to game. You need very little to score up 4♡ or 4♠.

We all know players who are constantly trying to convince the world of their bridge expertise. The value of those opinions can be summed up by the initials of the wonderful actress, Barbara Stanwyck. The truth is that bridge is easy to play, but **not easy** to play well. Every bridge player can learn to evaluate his hand more efficiently. It would even be fair to call that the essence of *points schmoints.*

The Real Truth About Distribution

Perhaps no other topic causes such controversy. Ask ten people, including teachers, and you could easily find yourself with ten distinct opinions. The time has come to clear the air.

There is bad distribution, good distribution and great distribution. The better your distribution the more you should bid. Here is the scoop.

Bad Distribution

4-3-3-3
> Bad for offense and defense, in both notrump and suit contracts.

5-3-3-2
> Bad offensively for suit contracts.

Excellent Distribution

5-4-3-1   **any 5-5**   **any 6-4**

---

* * *

Value of a Void in Suit Contract
After a Fit has been Found

Declarer   **3 points**

Dummy   **number of trumps**
> Five trumps = five points;
> Four trumps = four points, etc.

Value of a Singleton in Suit Contract
After a Fit has been Found

"Normal" two points, except...
> When dummy has at least four trumps, the singleton promotes to three points.

**Extra Points for Long Suits
in Notrump**

Add points as follows:
   Five-card suit   one point
   Six-card suit   three points
   Seven-card suit   five points

Add an additional point if you have a great suit, but subtract one for a poor suit.

**Extra Points for Long Suits
in Suit Contracts (presume a fit)**

Five-card suit   one, unless flat (5-3-3-2)

Six-card suit   three (but two if 6-3-2-2)

Seven-card suit   five (but four if 7-2-2-2)

Note: add one point for declarer's side suit if it is five cards long and a fit has been established.

There you are. Trust me, the above is quite accurate—it is definitely not inflated. All readers who apply this information will find themselves in makable contracts that their peers describe as "unbiddable."

Take a Second Look

You pick up your hand. You decide what you are going to open. Partner responds and now you are not so sure about where you are headed. Or partner opens, and you realize that your void in his suit is not quite as promising as it had been upon first glance. Now what?

In the next few pages we will look at hand evaluation from a different perspective than usual. We will learn how to reevaluate based on partner's actions. In each case, try to decide what you would bid before reading ahead. Note that each hand totals 14 HCP, but *points schmoints*.

For the first four hands, the auction proceeds:

West	North	East	South
1♠	P	2♠	P
???			

♠ AQ8642
♡ 7
◇ AKJ4
♣ 83

Bid 4♠. Nice hand! 20 points: 14 HCP, three points for your short suits, and three for length (one for the fifth spade, two additional for the sixth).

♠ Q8743
♡ QJ
◇ KQ73
♣ KJ

Yuck and double yuck. Pass and hope to make 2♠. You could add points for short suits and one point for the fifth spade after being supported. You must then subtract for the dubious club and heart honors as well as your aceless wonder. When the smoke finally clears, you are nowhere.

♠ A10642
♡ A5
◇ AQ83
♣ 74

You have your original 14 HCP, plus two for short suits and one for the fifth spade. The total is a healthy 17, and you should also be impressed with the three aces and the ♠10. Bid an invitational 3♠ (or 3◇) with absolutely no reservations.

A real *points schmoints* classic. Regardless of the formal total, you must bid 4♠ with this lovely hand after locating your fit.

For the next seven hands, partner opens 1NT (15-17) and it is your call:

West	North	East	South
1NT	P	???	

Pass. Where are you going? Your side has at most 25 points, and you lack the most underrated honor cards: aces and tens. Your trick-taking potential is also limited because a majority of your honors are in short suits. This hand with eight HCP would be a lot better:

♠ 73   ♡ 843   ◇ KQ108   ♣ QJ63

♠ 843
♡ 72
◇ AJ10874
♣ K7

Bid 3NT. If you are a slave to point count, you might believe that this hand is no better than the previous one. No way! Add three points for the diamond length and this becomes a clearcut raise to 3NT.

♠ 843
♡ 72
◇ A83
♣ KQ1062

Bid 3NT. With nine HCP, and an extra for your fifth club, 2NT would be inadequate.

Remember, partner opened 1NT (15-17).

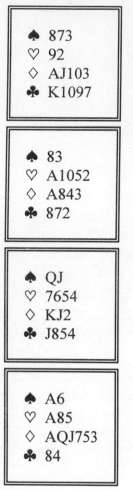

♠ 873
♥ 92
◇ AJ103
♣ K1097

Bid 2NT with this one. It is a great eight-count because of the five honors concentrated in your four-card suits. If you chose to jump all the way to 3NT, I would not think you were crazy.

♠ 83
♥ A1052
◇ A843
♣ 872

Bid 2♣. Even if partner does not bid hearts, you are quite ready to invite game with 2NT.

♠ QJ
♥ 7654
◇ KJ2
♣ J854

Pass. Your hand is ugly because its points are in its short suits. Your chances for game are negligible.

♠ A6
♥ A85
◇ AQJ753
♣ 84

Bid 6NT! With as many as eight tricks in your own hand, slam must be a good proposition. In the very unlikely event that you are off two club tricks, your direct approach provides no clue to your weak suit.

For the last four hands, the auction proceeds as follows:

West	North	East	South
1NT	P	2NT	P
???			

♠ QJ
♡ KJ7
◇ KQ32
♣ KJ52

pass, Pass, PASS. What trash! Personally, by the time I finished subtracting, I thought this hand was only worth 14 points.

♠ K6
♡ 843
◇ KQJ5
♣ AK109

Bid 3NT. This hand may resemble the previous one in distribution and HCP, but that is where the similarity ends. Your minor suits have superb trick-taking ability.

♠ A107
♡ A105
◇ 73
♣ AQJ108

Bid 3NT. You may have only 15 HCP, but you should treat this hand as an absolute maximum. You have aces, tens and a gorgeous five-card suit. At the risk of sounding like a teacher, any player not impressed by the ♣8 should be forced to trade it for the ◇8.

♠ KQ5
♡ K10754
◇ A8
♣ KJ7

Bid 3♡—a forcing bid which also shows your five-card suit. Correctly opening 1NT with this hand does not mean that you have no interest in your five-card major.

How did you fare? Do you need to reevaluate your reevaluating?

Quick Tricks—Out of Fashion?

It may be out of fashion to count quick tricks (also referred to as defensive tricks), but you cannot play good bridge without doing so. Many of your bidding decisions will be based on your quick-trick count, especially when considering whether or not to make a penalty double. The major benefit of counting quick tricks, however, is that it is an accurate way to evaluate your hand, because point count is often misleading.

The Official Encyclopedia of Bridge defines the quick trick as "a high card holding that in usual circumstances will win a trick by virtue of the rank of the cards in either offensive or defensive play."

In the days before point count, players evaluated their hands by counting their quick tricks—a sound practice.

Counting Quick Tricks	
AK in same suit	2 quick tricks
AQ in same suit	1 ½
A	1
KQ in same suit	1
Kx	½

Note that jacks are never "quick."

To give you an example of how counting quick tricks helps you to evaluate your hand properly, compare the following two hands using quick tricks as well as point count.

♠ AK98
♡ 64
♦ AQ73
♣ A74

This hand has 17 HCP. It also has **four and a half quick tricks** (two for the ♠AK, one and a half for the ◇ AQ and one for the ♣A).

♠ QJ64
♡ QJ
♦ AJ73
♣ KQJ

This hand also has 17 HCP. However, it has only two quick tricks: one each for the ◇A and the ♣KQ.

There is NO comparison between these two hands. The difference is magnified when considering play in a suit contract—sometimes "slow cards" are okay for play in notrump.

In case you are still in doubt, suppose you open 1NT with each of these hands and the auction continues:

You	Partner
1NT	2♣
2♠	3♠
???	

With the first hand, bid 4♠ like a shot. With the second, pass and pray that nine tricks might somehow materialize. Give partner a typical invitational 3♠ bid and you will appreciate the difference.

The following hand, played in the Grand National Teams in 1999, emphasizes the importance of proper hand evaluation.

```
                       North
                       ♠ 8
                       ♡ KJ832
                       ◇ 92
                       ♣ A9743
       West                              East
       ♠ Q942        ┌──────────┐        ♠ KJ3
       ♡ 75          │   4♡     │        ♡ 64
       ◇ K1087       │ ♣K LEAD  │        ◇ AQJ4
       ♣ KQJ         └──────────┘        ♣ 10642
                       South
                       ♠ A10765
                       ♡ AQ109
                       ◇ 653
                       ♣ 8
```

West	North	East	South
—	—	—	1♠
P	1NT	P	2♡
P	4♡	all pass	

(hand repeated for convenience)

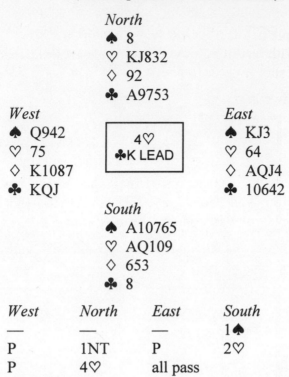

North
- ♠ 8
- ♡ KJ832
- ◇ 92
- ♣ A9753

West
- ♠ Q942
- ♡ 75
- ◇ K1087
- ♣ KQJ

4♡
♣K LEAD

East
- ♠ KJ3
- ♡ 64
- ◇ AQJ4
- ♣ 10642

South
- ♠ A10765
- ♡ AQ109
- ◇ 653
- ♣ 8

West	North	East	South
—	—	—	1♠
P	1NT	P	2♡
P	4♡	all pass	

South opened 1♠ based on The Rule of 20 (appreciating the two tens) and his two and a half quick tricks. Once North located the nice heart fit, he lost no time bidding the major-suit game.

The play presented no problems; South crossruffed for 11 tricks.

"What's the big deal?" you ask. "Did the declarer at the other table make the beginner's mistake of drawing trumps first?" No, he was a fine player. However, he was a point counter. At the other table, the hand was passed out!

*   *   *

She Does Not Go Both Ways

I use the same techniques for teaching hand evaluation in my classes as I do in my books. Arlene loved the idea of adding extra points for tens, for long suits, for just about anything. Her reaction was quite different when I taught her to subtract a point for a doubleton QJ. "No way, Marty. I am always happy to add, but I do **not** subtract."

The Good, the Fair...

A crucial principle of good bidding is: **with good hands, bid naturally, longest suit first**. With weak or mediocre hands, you must be practical. The following examples should serve to clarify this.

Compare these two hands:

Open 1◇ with the strong hand on the left. However, you must open 1♡ with the modest hand on the right. It is not strong enough for a 2♡ reverse after partner responds 1♠ to a 1◇ opening.

Now try these:

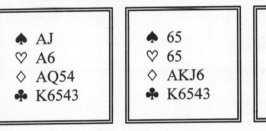

Open 1♣ with the first hand. With the middle hand, 1◇ is the correct bid because you will not be well placed if you open 1♣ and partner responds 1♡ or 1♠. With the last hand, open 1NT. It simply is not good enough for a 1♣ opening and 2◇ reverse. Although opening 1NT with two doubletons is imperfect, it is often the best strategy when your four-card suit is higher ranking than your five-bagger.

Select your opening bid with these two hands:

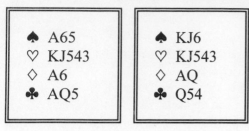

Open 1♡ with the hand on the left, but bid 1NT with the second hand. There is no way to show that you have a balanced hand with 16 HCP if you fail to open 1NT.

For the three hands that follow, you are West, the auction proceeds as indicated, and you must select your rebid.

West	North	East	South
1♣	P	1♠	P
???			

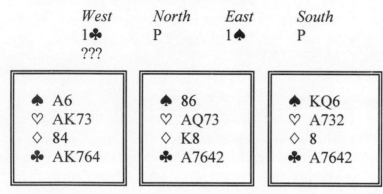

Bid 2♡ with the strong hand on the left, but choose 1NT with the second because you need a lot more to reverse. With the hand on the right, raise to 2♠—what else can you do?

Responder must also think ahead. For the remaining hands, you are East. Choose your bid.

West	North	East	South
1♣	P	???	

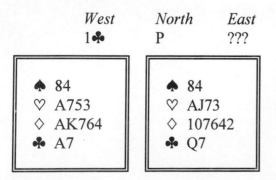

Respond 1♢ with the first hand and be prepared to bid your hearts next. With the second hand, bid 1♡ first, while it is easy to do so.

If you respond 1♢ (up-the-line) with the second hand, you will not be able to bid hearts later because your hand is simply too weak.

This time the auction proceeds:

West	North	East	South
1♡	P	???	

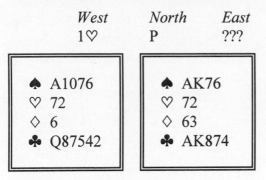

Remember the following: **if responder bids two suits, he virtually guarantees five cards in his first-bid suit**.

You must respond 1♠ with the first hand because you need a much better hand for a two-level response. 2♣ is your bid with the hand on the right. You will bid spades next, confident partner knows that you have only four cards in that suit.

In the final set of examples, partner's major outranks yours.

West	North	East	South
1♠	P	???	

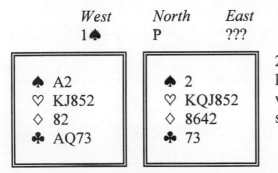

2♡ is fine with the hand on the left, but you must respond 1NT with the second hand, intending to show your hearts later.

I never have fun when I have to suppress my best suit. I always get a "wait, I forgot to tell you something" feeling. Okay, so I have the feeling. I get over it and look forward to getting good hands where I have the luxury of being able to "bid 'em up."

CHAPTER 3
Responder Takes Center Stage

Predicting Responder's First Bid

As legendary football coach Vince Lombardi once said, "failing to prepare is preparing to fail." In other words, thinking ahead is critical. In bridge, your ability to anticipate what partner is likely to respond will help you plan your auction. Let me tell it like it is: **When you open a minor, partner will probably respond in your shorter major. If you open 1♡ and are short in spades, partner will probably bid 1♠. Otherwise, when you open a major, partner will probably respond 1NT, whether or not you are playing 1NT Forcing.**

With the above in mind, plan your rebid with each of these hands after the expected response, and open accordingly.

Partner's likely response is 1♠.

Open 1◇, planning to raise to 2♠. You cannot do anything else. There are worse things in life than seven-card fits—they can be great character builders.

Partner's likely response is 1♠.

You are asking for trouble if you open 1♣. Plan ahead and open 1◇ so that when partner responds 1♠, you will have a painless 2♣ rebid. This sequence shows an opening bid with length in the minors.

Again, partner's likely response is 1♠.

An opening 1◇ bid would be going much too far. Open the obvious 1♣, intending to rebid 1NT.

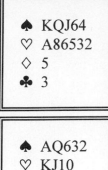

Partner's likely response is 1NT.

Open 1♠ so that you can rebid a comfortable 2♡. If you open 1♡ and partner responds 1NT, a reverse into spades will be asking for trouble. Partner will expect a much stronger hand.

Partner's likely response to 1♠ is 1NT.

Open 2NT. If you open 1♠, you do have an easy 3NT rebid. However, I cannot imagine any reason for you to risk being dummy.

♠ 6
♡ AKQJ
♢ AJ1065
♣ 742

Partner's likely response is 1♠.

In olden times, players opened 1♡ with hands like this. There was no sensible rebid if they opened 1♢ and partner responded 1♠. Modern players would sooner wash windows than open a four-card major in first or second seat. Perhaps I am getting old, but the auction...

West	North	East	South
1♡	P	1♠	P
2♢			

...is a lot more appealing than:

West	North	East	South
1♢	P	1♠	P
??? (argh)			

I open 1♡ and am proud to state it for the record.

Zeroing in on 1NT Forcing

A topic on everyone's mind is 1NT Forcing. Not only is this a staple for most duplicate junkies, but many social players have added it to their repertoire. Here are some questions that I have been asked over the years.

Dear Marty: Most of my friends play 1NT Forcing and love it. However, when someone explained the convention, I got confused. I have only been playing for three years and fancy bids are not easy for me. Any suggestions?

L. G., Hot Springs, Arkansas

Dear Not Easy: The two key concepts of 1NT Forcing are that responder can have 11 or even 12 HCP, and opener must bid again. It is not as radically different as some other conventions although many players have trouble with the followups.

Is this convention for everyone? Absolutely not. New players should never rush to add conventions simply because they are "in."

Dear Marty: I held a hand yesterday and I didn't know what to bid. I opened 1♡ with:

♠ KQ108   ♡ K9854   ◇ K4   ♣ J9

Partner responded 1NT Forcing. I knew that it would be wrong to reverse by bidding 2♠. I bid 2♡ but caught hell. What would you have done?

B.C., Hewlett, NY

Dear Rebid Problem: I have a lot of sympathy for your dilemma. If not playing 1NT Forcing, pass would be easy. A smattering of us are old enough to remember when four-card majors were opened. We bid 1♠ with hands like this which allowed us to make a painless 2♡ rebid.

Some modern players use a 2◇ opening bid as Flannery, promising a minimum opening bid with five hearts and four spades. That is perfect for hands like this one.

However, most players do not use Flannery. The Bergen solution is to treat 1NT as semi-forcing. Opener strives to find a bid, but is free to pass with minimum hands. Had I been in your shoes I guess I would have been forced to bid 2♣ (yuck).

Dear Marty: A friend told me that you do not love 1NT Forcing. Why don't you play 1NT nonforcing, showing 6-10 HCP?

Old Fashioned, Schenectady, NY

Dear Old Fashioned: As far as I am concerned, 1NT Forcing is not a great convention. When I open 1♠ with...

♠ Q8754   ♡ KQJ   ◇ J54   ♣ KJ

...and partner responds 1NT, I have no interest in taking another bid. We are not going anywhere. Even seven tricks may be too much with my minimum opening bid now that I know that responder's hand is limited. Playing 1NT Forcing, I would have to bid again and probably go down like a dog.

On the other hand, I love two-over-one game forcing. When responder is strong enough to show a new suit at the two level, it is a luxury for both players to know that we are going to game. Nobody is forced to jump or search for an artificial bid in order to get there.

Because it allows me to play two-over-one game forcing, my preferences for experienced players are:

1NT Semiforcing > 1NT Forcing > 1NT Nonforcing

Dear Marty: Two new controversies now exist in our club. Should 1NT be forcing by a passed hand? Should 1NT be forcing by responder in a competitive auction?

Bewildered in Boston

Dear Bewildered: NO. NO. 1NT Forcing should only be played when partner opens one of a major in first or second position and RHO passes.

Dear Marty: Yesterday I held:

♠ K63   ♡ K4   ◇ Q9754   ♣ QJ3

When my partner opened 1♠, I jumped to 3♠ as a limit raise. I was told that it was illegal to make this bid without four trumps. Am I in trouble?

Accused in Akron

Dear Accused: Absolutely not. First of all, it is important to appreciate the difference between illegal and unwise. In response to partner's 1♠ opening, the only illegal responses are insufficient bids such as 1♣, 1◇, 1♡ and 1♠ and the calls double and redouble. Even if you made the unwise response of 2♠, it is quite legal.

An invitational 3♠ bid with this hand is very logical. What your detractors were trying to say is that you should respond 1NT Forcing, planning to jump to 3♠ at your second turn. Bidding this way shows a limit raise with three trumps.

Any bridge player whose worst error is bidding 3♠ with the hand in question would be my idea of a great partner!

*   *   *

On the other hand, great partners are not always easy to find!

A little old man goes to the doctor and in the course of his physical, the doctor asks him, "are you an athlete?"

"Take a look at me, what do you think," Grandpa shoots back.

"Your shins and knees are all beat up, that's why I asked."

"No, no," says the old man. "I just play duplicate bridge with my wife."

Bergen Raises

This is the convention I will always be identified with. Bergen Raises complement five-card majors and are intended for experienced players. Bergen Raises are a byproduct of The Law of Total Tricks—we strive to get to the three level with nine trumps. The primary use of this convention occurs after partner opens 1♥ or 1♠ in first or second seat and RHO passes. (All numbers in the chart below include distribution.)

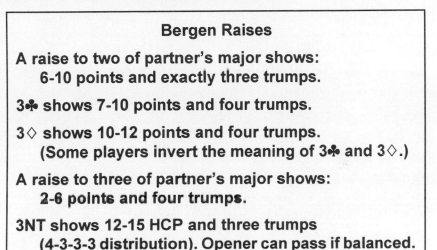

Bergen Raises

A raise to two of partner's major shows:
   6-10 points and exactly three trumps.

3♣ shows 7-10 points and four trumps.

3♦ shows 10-12 points and four trumps.
   (Some players invert the meaning of 3♣ and 3♦.)

A raise to three of partner's major shows:
   2-6 points and four trumps.

3NT shows 12-15 HCP and three trumps
   (4-3-3-3 distribution). Opener can pass if balanced.

All of the responses above are alertable when playing duplicate.

The following may be added to your arsenal as you see fit:

Jacoby 2NT, showing 13 or more points and four or more trumps.

1NT Forcing. A jump raise of opener's major at responder's second turn shows a three-card limit raise.

Now try bidding a few hands using Bergen Raises. Neither side is vulnerable. Partner opens 1♥.

♠ A53	♥ K732	◇ 76	♣ 8432	Respond 3♣.
♠ 8432	♥ Q632	◇ 83	♣ 632	3♥.
♠ A842	♥ K42	◇ 82	♣ J743	2♥.
♠ Q43	♥ J107	◇ A8532	♣ K7	1NT, then jump in hearts.
♠ KJ7	♥ J83	◇ Q743	♣ AK7	3NT.
♠ AK7	♥ KJ64	◇ 72	♣ K842	2NT.

Now partner opens 1♠.

♠ A83	♡ K843	◇ 63	♣ 7432	Respond 2♠.
♠ Q643	♡ Q843	◇ 52	♣ 732	3♠.
♠ A843	♡ K42	◇ 82	♣ J832	3♣.
♠ Q83	♡ J64	◇ A8532	♣ K7	1NT, then jump in spades.
♠ J75	♡ QJ3	◇ Q842	♣ AK7	3NT.
♠ AK5	♡ KJ76	◇ 72	♣ K743	2♣, then raise spades.
♠ A843	♡ A832	◇ Q7	♣ J73	3◇.

Although Bergen Raises work well in many auctions, there are times when they are not appropriate. The following should clarify the situation.

Most players do not use Bergen Raises as a passed hand, even if there is no competition. There are several reasons for this. Some players open four-card majors in third or fourth seat, so they cannot be assured of a nine-card fit when responder has four-card support. Drury (a convention described in the next article) allows responder to show his good raise at the two level. It is also true that the preemptive raise to the three level is not as useful when the opponents have chosen not to bid.

Take a look at what happens if the opponents have overcalled at the two level—it gets complicated. Although it is possible to incorporate Bergen raises in certain situations, my suggestion is to keep it simple and forego Bergen Raises when a jump to 3♣ is no longer possible. Notice that this need not apply if partner opens 1♡ and your RHO overcalls 1♠. You can elect to use the convention here.

If the opponents double partner's opening of 1♡ or 1♠, no problem! Use Bergen Raises as if the opponents had simply passed. I recommend this for both passed and unpassed hands.

In case you are curious, here is the origin of Bergen Raises.

In 1979 I played in my first national knockout final in the Grand National Teams in Las Vegas. My team was trailing when I picked up a hand I will never forget.

♠ J9654
♡ A5
◇ AK732
♣ 9

I opened 1♠ with both sides vulnerable. Partner raised to 2♠ while the opponents remained silent.

Not for the first or last time, I was in a quandary. Should I try for game? My great distribution and the vulnerable game bonus suggesting bidding, while the weak trumps and 12 HCP argued for a pass.

After much thought, I chose to pass, as did my LHO. The opening lead was made, and partner remarked as he tabled his hand: "I'm sure you did the right thing, Marty, I have a minimum."

Partner only had six HCP, but unfortunately, his "minimum" included the KQ107 of trumps! His exact hand was:

♠ KQ107   ♡ 9842   ◇ 85   ♣ J64

Of course, I made four easily, losing one trick each in spades, hearts and clubs. Worse than that, we lost the match.

Bridge players have to learn to live with bad results— they are inevitable, regardless of your experience or ability. However, this hand got me thinking. If only I had known about partner's four trumps, my decision would have been easy to make. In fact, as I continued to picture possible hands for partner, I became confident of one thing. Opposite a single raise with four trumps, my correct action was not merely to try for game, but to jump directly to 4♠.

Even if partner had as little as...

♠ A1087   ♡ 1062   ◇ 96   ♣ 8642

...game would be reasonable. Contrast that with a nice single raise with only three trumps, say...

♠ K73   ♡ Q1062   ◇ 94   ♣ K843

Now 4♠ would be no bargain. With a distributional hand like mine, the extra trump was everything.

What was the solution? I had never loved making strong jump shifts to the three level. Not only did they rarely occur, but they took up a great deal of bidding space. I could certainly live without them.

Shortly thereafter, the Bergen Raise of 3♣ was born. The finishing touches followed and soon we were ready to rock and roll.

An added bonus was the improved accuracy of our auctions after partner raised our major suit to two (obviously partner's most likely raise). The knowledge that partner could not have four trumps was extremely valuable. Any time that opener held a reasonable hand with weak trumps, he could take the low road once responder denied that magical ninth trump. We were now able to stop confidently at the two level when our opponents went overboard.

Duplicate players should note that if they are playing Bergen Raises, opener must alert the single raise (as well as the conventional responses). He knows that responder lacks a fourth trump and the opponents are entitled to that information. It might seem that alerting 1♡-P-2♡ is going too far, but when my opponents are playing Bergen Raises, I certainly want to know.

Each year, more and more players give Bergen Raises a try. They are quite precise and a lot of fun. If you are ready, go for it.

Drury—Anything but Dreary

You are playing at the local duplicate game where you and your partner are the acknowledged authorities, having won for three consecutive weeks.

♠ A87
♡ K942
◇ 86
♣ K743

West	North	East	South
P	P	1♠	P
???			

With a maximum passed hand in support of spades, you bid 3♠ and are a bit disappointed when partner passes. You are surprised when partner's usual "thank you" is not forthcoming after your dummy goes down and the contract fails.

Partner's hand is a perfectly normal third-seat opening:

♠ KQJ64   ♡ J85   ◇ A109   ♣ 95.

You conclude that it pays to be conservative after partner opens in third seat.

Everything goes smoothly for the next few rounds. Then you pick up:

♠ K864
♡ A873
◇ 92
♣ QJ3

West	North	East	South
P	P	1♠	P
???			

Having learned your lesson earlier, you bid only 2♠.

You confidently put down your dummy, but for some reason partner again does not seem pleased. He takes 11 tricks in rapid fashion, and you wonder why he did not invite game, which you would have been happy to accept. Partner chirps: "Do you really think I should have bid on with my hand?" He shows his cards.

♠ AJ1073   ♡ J   ◇ A754   ♣ K109

You are forced to admit that his pass cannot be criticized. However, you resolve that opener should be aggressive in these situations.

A few boards later, you pick up:

	West	North	East	South
♠ KQ1095	—	—	P	P
♡ Q	1♠	P	2♠	P
◇ A873	???			
♣ QJ8				

After partner raises to 2♠, and keeping your previous disaster in mind, you try for game with 3♠ which partner passes. Partner's hand is:

♠ 874   ♡ KJ942   ◇ Q104   ♣ 94

Despite the favorable location of the opponents' cards, you go down one, losing two clubs and one trick in each of the other suits. Partner, who has become less tolerant after each of your misadventures, bursts out with: "Can't you do anything right?" Although you can usually hold your own in a post-mortem, this time you find yourself at a loss for words.

The remainder of the session seems to drag on forever, and the spark has definitely left your partnership. You check your score and discover that you are two points below average, which has not happened in more than a year. You leave the club shortly after that, but not soon enough to avoid all the "What happened to the champs? They didn't win, and would you believe they were below average" remarks. The best of the lot: "Thanks for giving the rest of us a chance."

In an effort to interrupt the stone silence of the drive home, you say to partner, "Well, we'll get them next week."

"I don't think I can make it," he says. "I've got some very important shopping to do."

Lying awake that night, you think about the three fateful boards. It does not seem that you did anything terrible, yet in each situation your decision led to the wrong contract. Is there any solution to these problems?

All books on bidding advocate opening light in third seat. Many are deficient, however, in describing how responder should proceed after a third- or fourth-seat major-suit opener. Fortunately, one man recognized the problem and saw fit to propose a solution.

Douglas Drury was that man. He appreciated that using standard methods, the auction got too high when responder had a maximum passed hand with support. (Responder would jump to three of the major.) Drury's solution was for responder to bid 2♣ instead.

One reason that the Drury convention (named after Mr. Drury) is so desirable is its insignificant price tag. You merely give up a natural 2♣ response as a passed hand—no big deal. In 1982, your author refined Drury by introducing the use of 2◇ as another type of raise. After all, if you held a hand with good diamonds, such as...

♠ J4   ♡ QJ5   ◇ KQJ632   ♣ 85

...you would have opened 2◇.

Now there is a way to distinguish whether responder has three- or four-card support for opener's major. Bergen Two-Way Drury works like this:

Bergen Two-Way Drury

Partner opens a major in third or fourth seat.

Your RHO passes.

You bid 2♣ to show 10 or more distributional points with *exactly three* cards in partner's major.

or

You bid 2◇ to show 10 or more distributional points with *four* cards in partner's major.

Both the 2♣ and 2◇ bids are artificial and must be alerted because they say nothing about the suit you have bid.

Now let us see how the use of Bergen Two-Way Drury could have saved the day on the three problem hands from the duplicate game. You are West. Alertable bids are designated with an asterisk.

	West	East	
♠ A87	P	1♠	♠ KQJ64
♡ K942	2♣*	2♠	♡ J85
◇ 86	P		◇ A109
♣ K743			♣ 95

West's 2♣ bid promised a good passed hand with exactly three spades. East's 2♠ rebid said that he was not interested in game. West is now delighted to pass, having told his story. Opener's signoff in his trump suit with a minimum hand is called Reverse Drury. In original Drury, opener would have bid 2◇, which is outdated. When filling out your convention card, check the boxes in the major-suit opening section.

Here is the correct auction for our second problem hand:

	West	East	
♠ K864	P	1♠	♠ AJ1073
♡ A873	2◇*	4♠	♡ J
◇ 92	P		◇ A754
♣ QJ3			♣ K109

The 2◇ response shows a good passed hand while guaranteeing a fourth trump. That information is critical to opener with his distributional hand. If you believe that East's 4♠ bid is not warranted, here are a few other hands responder might have held. Game would be an excellent proposition with any one of them:

♠ 8654	♠ Q942	♠ 9854
♡ KQ94	♡ A109	♡ Q1087
◇ J2	◇ 2	◇ Q96
♣ A64	♣ Q8654	♣ AQ

Are you with me? I have no doubt that the ninth trump is analogous to the walk in baseball; it is the most underrated facet of the game.

Now for the last hand:

	West	East	
♠ KQ1095	—	P	♠ 874
♡ Q	1♠	2♠	♡ KJ942
◇ A873	P		◇ Q104
♣ QJ8			♣ 94

When East can only raise to 2♠, West passes, hoping to be able to take eight tricks.

Two-Way Reverse Drury is merely a fancy name for a convention that allows a pair to avoid annoying misguesses. The benefits of using it to clarify passed-hand auctions are important enough to appeal to any partnership.

Armed with Two-Way Reverse Drury, you can now rest assured that your partner will not be out shopping for a new partner.

CHAPTER 4
Opener Speaks Again

Opener Rebids With Six-Four

You open the bidding with attractive six-four distribution (remember, "six-four, bid more"). Partner responds and it is back to you. Now what?

In my experience, most players' instinct is to rebid their long suit. This is understandable; appreciating a long suit is good bridge. Unfortunately, repeating the six-bagger is usually not best. It is an inflexible approach. A more constructive way of bidding these hands is to show your four-card suit before you rebid your long suit. This is true whether the suits are majors or minors. My students remember this by chanting: "six-four-six".

Of course, there are exceptions, aren't there always? However, before considering those, let us take a look at the norm.

♠ AJ53	Open 1◇ and when partner responds 1♡, rebid 1♠, **not** 2◇. Your diamonds can wait.
♡ 83	
◇ AK7432	
♣ 5	

Open 1♡ and when partner responds 1♠, rebid 2◇, **not** 2♡. You hope to rebid your hearts later under the right circumstances.

♠ A8
♡ K86532
◇ KQJ6
♣ 4

Open 1♣ and when partner responds 1◇, rebid 1♡, **not** 2♣. Of course, if partner responds 1♠ instead of 1◇, you will rebid 2♣ to avoid reversing.

♠ 7
♡ KJ53
◇ A7
♣ KQ8432

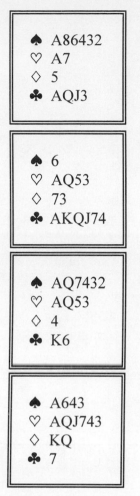

Open 1♠ and when partner responds 1NT, rebid 2♣, **not 2♠ or 3♠**.

♠ A86432
♡ A7
♢ 5
♣ AQJ3

Open 1♣ and when partner responds 1♠, rebid 2♡, **not 3♣**. Getting the idea?

♠ 6
♡ AQ53
♢ 73
♣ AKQJ74

Open 1♠ and when partner responds 1NT, rebid 2♡, **not 3♠**. I would also rebid 2♡ after partner's 2♣ or 2♢ response. Obviously, if partner raises to 2♠, you will ignore your hearts and bid 4♠.

♠ AQ7432
♡ AQ53
♢ 4
♣ K6

Open 1♡ and when partners responds 1NT, rebid 3♡, **not 2♠**. His 1NT bid denied four spades so there is no reason to bother showing that suit.

♠ A643
♡ AQJ743
♢ KQ
♣ 7

Now we are ready to consider the exceptions. We have already observed that it is sometimes right for opener to suppress his four-card suit. The thinking process is logical and does not require memorization.

There are two other situations that you should look at. In the first, your six-card suit is very strong and your four-card suit is shabby:

♠ KQJ1064
♡ 7532
♢ KQ
♣ K

Open 1♠ and when partner responds 1NT, rebid 2♠, **not 2♡**. With the disparity in suit quality, it feels more like seven-three distribution than six-four.

Finally, sometimes your values are so minimal that you are eager to limit your hand immediately.

♠ K5
♡ 7
♢ QJ10632
♣ AJ52

Open 1♢ and when partner responds 1♡, rebid 2♢, **not 2♣**. The 2♢ rebid limits you to a minimum hand, whereas a 2♣ rebid could be made with 17 points.

While exploring for the best contract, a considerate partner prefers to mention both of his suits. Six-four distribution is very nice, but on most hands do not forget to mention your four-card suit

Lacking Restraint

"Man who know not how to pass, often end up finishing last."

Anonymous

"Your first thought is your best answer." "Trust your instincts." That is what my high school teachers said when discussing strategy for my upcoming College Boards. Thirty-five years have gone by and I can tell you—that advice does not work as well in bridge.

Suppose you pick up:

♠ J65
♥ 85
◇ Q
♣ A1086532

You would like to show your club suit. Yet, if partner opens 1♥, 1◇ or 1♠, you must exercise restraint. You cannot bid clubs because you are not strong enough to respond at the two level. If partner opens 1♠ raise to 2♠; bid 1NT over 1♥ or 1◇.

♠ 74
♥ 53
◇ AKQJ104
♣ 632

What a great diamond suit. What could be more obvious than showing your 24-carat diamonds? After partner opens 1NT, however, the sensible response is a raise to 3NT.

What do you think when you have AKQ542 in a suit? That holding would make anyone's list of rebiddable suits—who would not repeat a suit like that? On the next hand, my partner was eager to tell me about his great hearts. The result of his impulsiveness, was two delighted opponents.

North (Marty)
♠ 9765
♥ 7
◇ 10753
♣ QJ109

West
♠ AJ10
♥ J10986
◇ Q
♣ AK52

```
┌─────────────┐
│ 2♥ DBL      │
│ ♣A LEAD     │
└─────────────┘
```

East
♠ Q43
♥ 3
◇ AKJ92
♣ 7643

South
♠ K82
♥ AKQ542
◇ 864
♣ 8

West	North	East	South
—	—	P	1♥
P	P	2◇	2♥
Dbl	all pass		

It is easy to see what happened to the ill-fated 2♥ bid, but was this bad luck or bad bridge? South knew that I held fewer than six points when I passed 1♥. East had passed originally; he was just balancing. West had to have a very good hand. After all, the points had to be somewhere. Why had West passed 1♥?

The answer to this mystery is always the same. The only reason for passing with a good hand is that you have length (and usually strength) in the opponent's suit. It was dollars to donuts that West had a trap pass of hearts! And wasn't South obliging! He did not just fall into the trap, he dove in head first. East was delighted to leave West's penalty double in—not only did he have a maximum passed hand, he even held a trump.

How bad was 2♥ doubled? Suffice it to say that when the smoke cleared, South had taken only four tricks, resulting in 1100 points for East-West.

South looked like he did not know what had hit him. I could not think of anything soothing to say. In the interest of partnership harmony I mumbled something like: "Sorry I didn't have a better hand."

Next time you think that you **have** to bid, remember: bridge may be a bidder's game, but sometimes, "discretion is the better part of valor."

Opener's Obscure Rebid

Opener's second bid is often critical, but not clearcut. Here are some typical rebid decisions that you might be confronted with at the table. For all nine hands, the opponents are silent. You open 1♣ and partner responds 1♠. Now what?

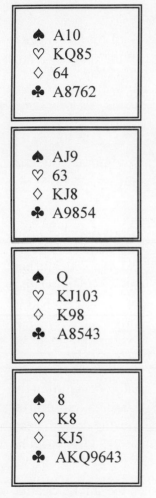

♠ A10
♡ KQ85
◊ 64
♣ A8762

Bid 1NT. You have no alternative. This may not be pretty, but 2♡ shows a big hand, and I consider 2♣ to be quite obscene.

♠ AJ9
♡ 63
◊ KJ8
♣ A9854

Raise to 2♠. Many players refuse to raise with only three trumps here. They would rebid 2♣ or 1NT—so much for them. As for me, I will be delighted to play in spades even though partner may have only four.

♠ Q
♡ KJ103
◊ K98
♣ A8543

Bid 1NT. Once again, you have little choice. At least your singleton spade is an honor.

♠ 8
♡ K8
◊ KJ5
♣ AKQ9643

Bid 3NT, which is what you expect to make after partner's 1♠ response. This rebid always promises great length in the suit you opened.

Remember, you opened 1♣ and partner responded 1♠.

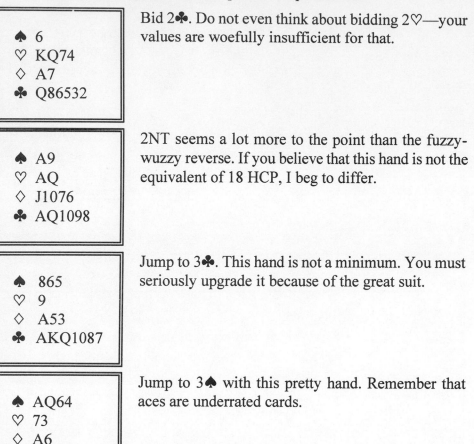

♠ 6
♡ KQ74
◇ A7
♣ Q86532

Bid 2♣. Do not even think about bidding 2♡—your values are woefully insufficient for that.

♠ A9
♡ AQ
◇ J1076
♣ AQ1098

2NT seems a lot more to the point than the fuzzy-wuzzy reverse. If you believe that this hand is not the equivalent of 18 HCP, I beg to differ.

♠ 865
♡ 9
◇ A53
♣ AKQ1087

Jump to 3♣. This hand is not a minimum. You must seriously upgrade it because of the great suit.

♠ AQ64
♡ 73
◇ A6
♣ A10743

Jump to 3♠ with this pretty hand. Remember that aces are underrated cards.

I will conclude with a classic *points schmoints* hand.

♠ Q762
♡ QJ
◇ KJ
♣ KQJ53

Yuck! How ugly can we get? 2♠ is enough. This hand has a grand total of one and a half quick tricks. Contrast this with the preceding hand. If you were playing for money, which would you rather have?

CHAPTER 5
Bridge is a Partnership Game

Forcing or Not?

It is important to know when partner makes a forcing bid. This is not an easy topic to master. Can you prove me wrong?

For each example, state whether or not the last bid is forcing. The opponents' actions are included, be sure to notice them.

West	North	East	South
1♡	P	1♠	P
2♣			

This is not a forcing bid. If opener had wanted to force, he could have jump shifted to 3♣. Responder would pass 2♣ holding:

♠ Q743   ♡ 7   ◇ A8642   ♣ 743

West	North	East	South
1◇	P	1♠	P
2♡			

The reverse is forcing. Opener could have a great hand such as:

♠ AK7   ♡ AJ74   ◇ AK854   ♣ 6

West	North	East	South
1♡	P	1♠	P
2◇	P	3♡	

Not forcing. Responder has an invitational hand like:

♠ KQ1074   ♡ 743   ◇ AJ   ♣ J83

West	North	East	South
1◇	P	2◇	P
2♡			

Forcing. Opener's bid shows the equivalent of a reverse. He is exploring for the best contract even though responder has a weak hand and has denied a four-card major.

West	North	East	South
3♣	P	3♠	

Forcing. A new suit after partner's two- or three-level preempt is considered forcing. Responder could have a big hand such as:

♠ AQ8432   ♡ 7   ◇ AKJ4   ♣ K4

West	North	East	South
1◇	P	1♠	P
2◇	P	2♡	

Forcing, just as a new suit by an "unpassed" responder usually is. Responder might have:

♠ AQ832   ♡ AJ83   ◇ Q6   ♣ 94

West	North	East	South
1♣	P	1♠	P
1NT	P	2♡	

This auction is not forcing. After opener rebids 1NT, responder's bid in a lower suit shows a weak distributional hand. He is escaping from notrump with something like:

♠ Q8432   ♡ KJ742   ◇ 82   ♣ 4

West	North	East	South
1◇	P	3♡	

This is not forcing. The double jump shows a very weak hand, perhaps:

♠ 7   ♡ KQ108542   ◇ 63   ♣ 842

West	North	East	South
1◇	P	1♡	P
3◇	P	3♡	

Forcing. Once responder does not pass opener's invitational jump, the partnership is forced to game.

West	North	East	South
P	P	1♣	P
1♡			

Not forcing by the passed hand.

West	North	East	South
P	P	1◇	P
1♡	P	**2NT**	

Not forcing, whether or not West was a passed hand. East has 18-19 HCP.

West	North	East	South
P	P	1♣	P
1♡	P	**2♠**	

Forcing. The game-forcing jump shift is not affected by the fact that West is a passed hand.

West	North	East	South
1♡	Dbl	P	2♣
P	**2♠**		

Not forcing. North has a big hand, but partner can pass with nothing. I would bid this way holding:

♠ AK875 ♡ 4 ◇ AQJ8 ♣ A74

West	North	East	South
1◇	1♠	P	**2♣**

Not forcing after the overcall. South might hold:

♠ 7 ♡ A843 ◇ 73 ♣ KQ8654

West	North	East	South
3♣	Dbl	P	3♠
P	4◇		

Not forcing. At the four level, North might hold a very good hand, but if South is broke, he can pass. North might even be as good as:

♠ Q84   ♡ AK32   ◇ AKQ92   ♣ 7

West	North	East	South
1◇	1NT	2♡	

Not forcing. East should have a weak hand with long hearts. With anything more, he should make a penalty double of 1NT.

West	North	East	South
1NT	2♠	3♣	

Not forcing. Responder is only competing against 2♠. He could have:

♠ 7   ♡ 8532   ◇ 73   ♣ QJ10642

West	North	East	South
1♡	2◇	Dbl	P
2♡	P	3♣	

The double is negative. The 3♣ bid is not forcing. East has a weak club-oriented hand with spades on the side such as:

♠ K742   ♡ —   ◇ 842   ♣ KJ10953

West	North	East	South
1◇	1♠	Dbl	P
3♣			

Not forcing. If opener had a game-forcing hand, he would have cuebid 2♠.

Now that you know all the answers, why not buy your partner this book so he will be as smart as you?

Good Partnership Bidding

Most players can handle the first few bids of a noncompetitive auction. Very often, the challenge occurs later. Each of these five hands begins with the same three bids. After that, it is time to distinguish **bridge players** from bridge players.

		West	*East*		
♠	6	1◇	1♡	♠	832
♡	J52	2♣	2◇	♡	AQ1063
◇	AKJ52	2♡	4♡	◇	Q74
♣	AQ74	P		♣	83

This intelligent auction led to the best contract. After West showed his clubs, East had no choice but to take a preference to partner's first suit.

West now bid 2♡ because he knew: **when opener has three-card support for responder's major, he must show it at some point because responder might have five.** He dared not bid any higher because East had shown a weak hand.

East was delighted to land in hearts, and took a second look at his modest hand. He appreciated his four red-suit honors and deduced that partner was short in spades. He now lost no time bidding the excellent major-suit game.

		West	*East*		
♠	QJ7	1◇	1♡	♠	842
♡	6	2♣	2♡	♡	KQJ842
◇	AK743	P		◇	6
♣	AJ73			♣	854

West had a nice hand, but the auction did not go his way. After East could do no more than repeat his suit at the two level, West made a restrained pass. A 2NT rescue bid would have been a grave mistake.

		West	*East*		
♠	73	1◇	1♡	♠	QJ6
♡	Q	2♣	3♡	♡	AKJ742
◇	AJ8532	4♡	P	◇	76
♣	AKJ6			♣	93

Note West's 2♣ bid. With six-four distribution, he correctly showed his four-card suit at his second turn to bid.

After East's invitational 3♡ bid, West was able to use a Bergenism: **when partner has shown a six-card suit, a singleton honor is equivalent to two small cards,** and raised accordingly.

		West	*East*		
♠	742	1◇	1♡	♠	K63
♡	8	2♣	3NT	♡	AQ74
◇	AKQ6	P		◇	J83
♣	K8532			♣	A74

West showed good foresight with his opening bid of 1◇. Opener would have been in trouble if he had opened 1♣ and partner had responded 1♡.

East had no reason to fool around and jumped to 3NT.

		West	*East*		
♠	6	1◇	1♡	♠	K73
♡	J73	2♣	2♠*	♡	KQ954
◇	AK763	3♡	4♡	◇	Q5
♣	AQ53	P		♣	K86

After our inevitable start, East appreciated the possibility of playing in hearts if West had three-card support. He probed with 2♠, fourth-suit forcing to game, rather than plunge into 3NT. Once West supported hearts, East knew just what to do.

Careful planning in the auction can go a long way. Better to be good than hope to be lucky!

To Rebid or Not to Rebid?

What question am I asked more than any other? That is easy: "Marty, should I repeat a five-card suit?"

The short answer is "not usually." For example, as East you hold:

	West	North	East	South
♠ AJ754	1◇	P	1♠	P
♡ J52	1NT	P	???	
◇ 7643				
♣ 8				

Bid 2◇, not 2♠. Opener could hold:

♠ Q   ♡ AK106   ◇ Q9852   ♣ K72

How about the following? Once again you are East.

	West	North	East	South
♠ A4	1◇	P	1♡	P
♡ K10852	1♠	P	???	
◇ 76				
♣ 9864				

You should bid 1NT, not 2♡. Suppose partner has:

♠ KQ93   ♡ 7   ◇ AQ853   ♣ J72

However, there are specific situations when rebidding a five-card suit is acceptable and even necessary. Any time that your suit has been supported, it is okay to rebid it without concern. Here are two examples (you are West):

	West	North	East	South
♠ 9	1◇	Dbl	2◇	2♠
♡ AK85	???			
◇ K9876				
♣ K83				

It is clear to compete to 3◇. Not only is it likely that you will make this, but it would be criminal to allow the enemy to play a cozy 2♠.

	West	North	East	South
♠ KQJ63	1♠	P	2♠	P
♡ 9	???			
◇ KQJ				
♣ AQ75				

Jump to 4♠ without a second thought.

Other exceptions follow specific guidelines:

**When to Rebid
an Unsupported Five-Card Suit**

After partner has promised two or more cards in the suit.

In the middle of a forcing auction.

When forced to bid in a competitive auction.

Note that in all the examples that follow, the suit you are rebidding has some meat on its bones. In the first two, the 1NT bid promises at least two cards in partner's suit.

	West	*North*	*East*	*South*
♠ 75	1♣	P	1NT	P
♡ KQJ7	???			
◇ 86				
♣ KQJ53				

2♣ will be a much better contract than 1NT.

	West	*North*	*East*	*South*
♠ 75	1◇	P	1♡	P
♡ QJ973	1NT	P	???	
◇ K6				
♣ 9853				

Bid 2♡ to play in a known seven-card fit. Your hearts will be worth more in that contract than in notrump.

On the next three hands, there is a common theme. Partner cannot drop you in a bad spot because he is forced to bid again. You can follow a very sound bidding principle in each case: **when in doubt, make the cheapest plausible bid**. Partner's next bid will clarify the situation.

	West	*North*	*East*	*South*
♠ 96	1♡	P	2◇	P
♡ KQJ87	???			
◇ AK				
♣ 9864				

Bid 2♡, no other bid is worth discussing.

	West	North	East	South
♠ A	1♡	P	1♠	P
♡ AKJ74	2♣	P	2◇*	P
◇ 743	???			
♣ J987				

* Fourth-suit forcing to game.

Bid 2♡. Because 2◇ was an artificial bid, you would need a diamond stopper to bid notrump.

	West	North	East	South
♠ KQ974	1◇	P	1♠	P
♡ K5	2♡	P	???	
◇ 76				
♣ 8754				

Bid 2♠. See what partner does next.

You are not thrilled to rebid three of your minor with either of the following hands, but there is no better option. **After the opponents have bid, you need a stopper in their suit to bid notrump**. The imperfect rebid is the lesser of evils with these two hands:

	West	North	East	South
♠ 8765	1◇	2♠	Dbl	P
♡ AK	???			
◇ QJ1043				
♣ K6				

Dbl is negative.

Bid 3◇. Absolutely no alternative.

	West	North	East	South
♠ 864	1♣	1♠	2♡	P
♡ 75	???			
◇ AKJ				
♣ KJ1097				

Bid 3♣. No other choice is possible.

I hope that I was able to shed some light on this important topic. These exceptions are certainly valid, but they are exceptions. If you usually avoid rebidding five-card suits, you are doing just fine.

After You Pass, Tread Lightly

What went wrong with these auctions from actual play? On every hand, the result was down one.

Everyone knows that you can open light when partner is a passed hand. Following up correctly is not always so easy. Take a look at five auctions where a partnership fell from grace.

	West	East	
♠ 10754	P	1♦	♠ KJ6
♡ AQ6	1♠	2♠	♡ K975
◇ Q	P		◇ KJ632
♣ J9843			♣ Q

If East had dealt, I would agree with his bidding. However, once West passed, East was under no obligation to find a rebid. When West did not respond in hearts, East should have dismissed all thoughts of game and passed 1♠.

	West	East	
♠ A83	P	1♦	♠ KJ4
♡ AJ32	1♡	1NT	♡ 85
◇ J8	2NT	P	◇ A7643
♣ J632			♣ K75

I agree with East's bidding. What else could he do? His rebid showed fewer than 15 HCP, and in third seat he could have a lot less. There was **no** chance that the partnership had 26 points, so West should have passed 1NT; even that modest contract is not easy to make. Hands with a lot of jacks are not as good as they look.

	West	East	
♠ Q10653	P	1♣	♠ J742
♡ AK973	1♠	2♠	♡ QJ
◇ 10	4♠	P	◇ KJ3
♣ 95			♣ KQ107

I have no quarrel with West's bidding; his hand was looking mighty good after partner opened and raised. The culprit was East, who should have passed 1♠—where was he going? He was certainly right to be pleased after West responded in spades, but should have realized that game was not possible opposite a passed hand.

	West	East	
♠ KQ87	P	1◇	♠ A
♡ A1054	1♡	2♣	♡ J32
◇ 43	2NT	P	◇ KJ765
♣ Q54			♣ K973

West's hand could have appeared in a textbook, illustrating a perfect 2NT rebid over 2♣. Once again, East was unrealistic. He should have been delighted that his partner responded in his longer major and passed 1♡. When your partner cannot open, and your hand is mediocre, stop bidding as soon as possible.

	West	East	
♠ 73	P	1♠	♠ AQ654
♡ KJ865	2♡	3◇	♡ 102
◇ A6	3NT	P	◇ KJ752
♣ Q987			♣ K

Many pairs would duplicate this auction. I am sorry, but I cannot agree. East's nice shape offered hope for a spade game even after West's initial pass. Once West failed to support spades, however, East had to be realistic and stay low. After West showed his five hearts, East should pass 2♡, content to stop in a reasonable contract.

Get the point? After one player has passed, both partners must be on their toes. I am not saying that you should forget about game, but I am saying that passed-hand auctions must be handled with care.

CHAPTER 6
Notrump Bidding for the Millennium

1NT—To Open or Not To Open?

If the answer to this question seems obvious to you, please read on. I am not inquiring as to what notrump range you play. Our frame of reference is the standard 15-17 HCP. Perhaps you think I am going to bore you by asking what you should open with:

♠ AJ7   ♡ KJ94   ◇ A63   ♣ K74

That is not going to happen. Keep in mind that leopards never change their spots; I am far more subtle than that.

A few words of warning before you read on.

I **love** long suits, aces, kings and tens.
I **do not love** queens, jacks, 4-3-3-3 shape or honors in short suits.
I **hate** rebid problems that could have been avoided.

Ready or not, here goes. For each hand, the only question is: do you open 1NT or don't you? Cover up the answer to the right **before** you decide what action you would take.

♠ 75
♡ KJ104
◇ AKQ10
♣ A107

No. If you consider this hand to be worth 17 points for notrump, then you believe that tens should be evaluated the same as deuces. Sorry, I cannot agree. Everyone can see that this hand would be too good for an opening 1NT if the ♠7 were replaced with the jack. Personally, I would rather have those three lovely tens.

♠ AQ
♡ K63
◇ AQ
♣ 976543

For sure. Opening 1NT describes this hand much better than opening 1♣ and rebidding 2♣. Your weak club suit and great stoppers argue for opening 1NT despite you two doubletons.

♠ QJ
♥ QJ64
◇ KQJ
♣ QJ63

No. You may consider this collection worth 15 points—to me it is just a pile of garbage. With your one measly quick trick, open 1♣ instead.

♠ K63
♥ A105
◇ AQJ104
♣ 83

Yes! With the gorgeous five-card diamond suit and two tens, this is a lovely hand. Is it inconsistent to say that 14 HCP can be worth more than 15? If you were playing high-stakes rubber bridge, would you rather pick up this hand or the one directly above? No contest, this hand wins in a landslide.

♠ AJ109
♥ A7
◇ A76
♣ A643

No. I was taught many years ago that four aces should be counted as 17. My experience over the years has reinforced that concept. This hand is simply too good for a 1NT opening.

♠ K6
♥ AJ75
◇ KJ987
♣ K3

Yes. You would be very uncomfortable if you opened 1◇ and partner responded 1♠. Avoid that problem by getting your values off your chest. You will have an easy rebid if you open 1NT.

♠ A64
♥ AQ1094
◇ A63
♣ K5

Not this one. The beautiful five-card suit makes it too good for a 15-17 1NT opening. I am delighted to call this an 18-point hand.

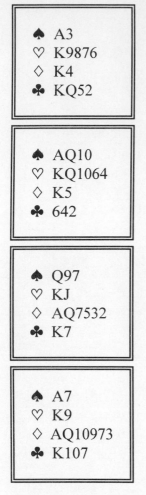

♠ A3
♡ K9876
♢ K4
♣ KQ52

Another no. When a hand has five-four distribution and the five-card suit is higher ranking than the second suit, you never have to open 1NT. Open 1♡.

♠ AQ10
♡ KQ1064
♢ K5
♣ 642

The fifth heart and two tens definitely make this hand strong enough for a 1NT opening. I predict that this answer will be especially unpopular.

♠ Q97
♡ KJ
♢ AQ7532
♣ K7

Yes. A 1NT opening describes this hand better than any other action.

♠ A7
♡ K9
♢ AQ10973
♣ K107

No. With your pretty six-card diamond suit and prime cards, this hand is much too strong for a 1NT opening.

Please do not worry if you did not like many of my answers—I bet you are not alone. On the other hand, good bidding involves a lot more than counting HCP. The easiest way to advance your bridge level is to learn the proper way to evaluate the cards you are dealt.

Secrets for Responding to 1NT

Partner opens 1NT. Great! What are your thoughts? Among others, you might wonder what suit will become trump. Will you play in notrump? How high will you go? The answers to these questions will become easier to attain if you assign your hand its proper evaluation. Your opening notrump range is 15-17, but these concepts are equally applicable to other ranges.

If you have 4-3-3-3 distribution including a four-card major, do not bother with Stayman. Just bid the appropriate number of notrump. Decide what you would do with each hand, then look to the right for the answer.

| ♠ QJ75 ♡ KJ4 ◇ K82 ♣ Q74 | Raise to 3NT. |
| ♠ K53 ♡ Q742 ◇ Q54 ♣ Q105 | Invite by bidding 2NT. |

Do not forget to add points for long suits. The next three hands are not equal even though they each contain identical honor cards.

♠ 743 ♡ 8742 ◇ AJ10 ♣ K53	Pass.
♠ 74 ♡ 842 ◇ AJ1076 ♣ K53	Bid 2NT.
♠ 74 ♡ 84 ◇ AJ10763 ♣ K53	Bid 3NT.

If you have a nondescript eight points, pass. This includes hands with four-card majors. Game is unlikely—you should just take your plus score. If you are lucky and make nine tricks, that is not bad at any form of scoring. **Pass** partner's opening 1NT with both of these hands:

♠ Q84 ♡ Q73 ◇ K753 ♣ J32

♠ Q7 ♡ 8642 ◇ Q853 ♣ KJ7

On the next three hands, remember to appreciate your spot cards.

♠ J7 ♡ A64 ◇ K732 ♣ 8532	Pass.
♠ J73 ♡ 64 ◇ A1032 ♣ K1092	Raise to 2NT.
♠ 1093 ♡ 64 ◇ A1098 ♣ KJ109	Bid 3NT.

(Bid 3♣ if playing Puppet Stayman.)

Most of these secrets reflect good hand evaluation. If you did not fare too well, you should review Chapter 2. Not everyone can play bridge like the experts, but their bidding secrets are now fair game.

Puppet Stayman Made Easy

In *Points Schmoints!* I strongly recommended opening 1NT with balanced hands that include a five-card major. Nothing that has happened since has even suggested that this is bad strategy.

I mentioned in passing that there was a convention called Puppet Stayman that would allow responder to uncover that five-card major.

After numerous inquiries, the time has come to discuss the subject in detail. **Please keep in mind that opening 1NT with a five-card major is a long-range winning proposition**, whether or not you use Puppet Stayman. Of course, it is nice to be able to have your cake and eat it too.

If you decide to try the convention, you need not rush to do it all at once. Simplify and modify it based on practical considerations for your partnership.

Puppet Stayman

When opener bids 1NT, 3♣ by responder promises a game-forcing hand (ten or more HCP) with at least one three-card major.

Responder may also have exactly one four-card major. He should not bid this way with 4-3-3-3 distribution, or with a five-card major.

The 3♣ response is artificial and alertable. A correct explanation by opener would be: "Responder has a game-going hand with at least one three-card major." Because opener was asked if he has a five-card major, his 3♡ and 3♠ responses show five cards in those suits.

When opener does not have a five-card major, he asks himself, "Do I have a four-card major?" If not, he bids 3NT. The 3NT bid says "I do not have a four- or five-card major. Enough questions. Stop bothering me and let me play 3NT."

If opener has one or two four-card majors, he rebids 3◇.

Opener's Responses to Puppet Stayman

3♡ and 3♠ show five cards in the bid major.

3NT denies any four- or five-card major.

3◇ shows one or two four-card major(s).

All of opener's rebids are alertable.

If responder has no four-card major, he will always know exactly what to do. When he does have one four-card major, he will explore further after opener rebids 3◇. Everyone agrees that it is nice to have the strong hand declare. Therefore, responder's search for a four-four major-suit fit forces him to act like a rebellious teenager—he bids the major he does not have. Take a look at an example sequence. (An asterisk denotes an alertable bid.)

Opener	Responder
1NT	3♣*
3◇*	3♡*

> Opener alerts the 3♡ bid and explains that responder is showing a four-card spade suit. This is not a transfer, it is merely a description. Obviously, opener will bid spades if he has four; otherwise, he will retreat to 3NT.

If you are overwhelmed, not to worry. The following examples should prove useful in cementing your understanding of Puppet Stayman.

	Opener	Responder	
♠ K7532	1NT	3♣*	♠ QJ6
♡ KQ6	3♠*	4♠	♡ 93
◇ AQ	P		◇ J9743
♣ Q43			♣ AK9

Opener's 1NT described his hand very nicely. Responder had enough strength to bid 3NT, but 4♠ would be preferable if partner had five of them. Voilà.

	Opener	Responder	
♠ K643	1NT	3♣*	♠ A98
♡ AQ76	3◇*	3NT	♡ K54
◇ K9	P		◇ A8762
♣ AJ10			♣ 98

On this hand, responder is interested in a five-three fit in either major. When opener denies a five-card major, responder signs off in the normal contract of 3NT.

		Opener	*Responder*		
♠	K72	1NT	3♣*	♠	A98
♡	J9876	3♡*	3NT	♡	K
◇	AJ	P		◇	965
♣	AQ6			♣	K98742

Responder knew better than to bother with his clubs. However, a five-three spade fit was worth looking for. When opener showed his five hearts, responder lost no time bidding the cheapest game.

		Opener	*Responder*		
♠	1043	1NT	3♣*	♠	K
♡	KQ876	3♡*	4♡	♡	AJ9
◇	KJ	P		◇	862
♣	AQ10			♣	K98742

If at first you don't succeed....This time, opener's five-card major was music to responder's ear.

		Opener	*Responder*		
♠	AK43	1NT	3♣*	♠	Q987
♡	AQ4	3◇*	3♡*	♡	K63
◇	K86	3♠	4♠	◇	AQ72
♣	543	P		♣	98

Responder prefers Puppet Stayman to a 2♣ response in case opener has five hearts. When opener promises a four-card major (while denying five), responder checks for the four-four spade fit by bidding 3♡. When he hears the good news, he is happy to bid 4♠.

		Opener	*Responder*		
♠	AK7	1NT	3♣*	♠	Q984
♡	AQ54	3◇*	3♡*	♡	K76
◇	983	3NT	P	◇	AQ62
♣	K97			♣	84

When no eight-card major-suit fit is found, the pair settles in 3NT.

Puppet gains in many auctions and breaks even in others. Sounds like my kind of odds.

Crawling Stayman

I can just hear you thinking. "Marty, you must be kidding. In the beginning, there was Stayman. In *Points Schmoints!* you taught us Garbage Stayman. You touched on Puppet Stayman in that book, and you have clarified that subject in this book. Now you hit me with another variation?"

Patience, dear readers. I think you will find this one to be quite palatable. Please hear me out. I will begin with a couple of examples. You have the following hand and partner opens 1NT:

♠ J7643
♡ J7643
◇ 5
♣ 94

You know that your weak, distributional hand will play better in a suit than in notrump. You are playing Jacoby transfers, so you can even arrange for partner to declare.

The problem here is that even those of you who are blessed with extraordinary intuition have no idea which major partner prefers. How would you feel if you transferred to hearts and partner produced the following?

♠ KQ92   ♡ 92   ◇ AQ87   ♣ A85

Yes, 2♠ would make easily, while 2♡ would probably go down. My idea of a good trump fit is not J7643 opposite 92.

Obviously if you choose to transfer to spades, partner might hate spades and love hearts. There is just no way for you to know.

Playing "regular" Stayman, you will do just fine when partner shows that he has a four-card major. However, if he bids 2◇, you will be lost. Because you are unprepared to play there, you have the same problem with Garbage Stayman. With this hand, Crawling Stayman is the only form of the convention that leaves you in good shape when partner denies a major.

If you are willing to adopt my suggestion, you will do the following. Inform your favorite partner that you would like to try playing "Crawling Stayman." Explain that after the auction begins 1NT-2♣-2◇, responder's 2♡ bid promises a weak hand with both majors (if responder only had hearts, he would simply have transferred). When playing duplicate, opener must alert responder's 2♡ rebid.

Once responder crawls to 2♡, opener's life is easy. With three cards in one major and two in the other, he need only place the contract in his longer major. If opener has three cards in each, he will usually bid 2♠ so that he becomes declarer. Of course, when opener's hearts are much stronger, he is welcome to pass 2♡.

Once responder crawls to 2♡, he is stating that game is out of the question. In fact, his crawl promises no strength. I would be delighted to use Crawling Stayman holding:

♠ 65432   ♡ 65432   ◇ 2   ♣ 32.

Are you still with me? I will not be insulted if you have turned the page already, but my students do not believe that this is a convention for experts only. Of course, we all know players who could be described as stubborn traditionalists. They would sooner give up dessert than respond Stayman with fewer than eight points. They will not be any more impressed with Crawling Stayman than they were with Garbage Stayman. Of course, **you** are much more enlightened.

I have always believed that examples are worth more than a thousand words. I hope that you will agree.

		West	*East*		
♠	AJ4	1NT	2♣	♠	K1098
♡	K4	2◇	2♡*	♡	97532
◇	KJ65	2♠	P	◇	8
♣	KQ53			♣	974

Notice that you need not wait for five-five distribution to use Crawling Stayman. As long as responder is interested in both majors, Crawling Stayman is the way to go. With your five lousy hearts, it is nice to bring a second suit into the picture.

		West	*East*		
♠	K5	1NT	2♡*	♠	QJ1097
♡	A98	2♠	P	♡	6532
◇	AQ64			◇	107
♣	K943			♣	75

With the solid spades, responder ignores his anemic hearts.

	West	East	
♠ Q52	1NT	2♣	♠ J1098
♡ AK8	2◇	2♡*	♡ QJ107
◇ 10854	P		◇ 7
♣ AK6			♣ 9543

It is rare to crawl with four-four, but the chunky suits and singleton diamond make this the indicated action. Opener passes 2♡ because his hearts are so strong.

	West	East	
♠ AQ63	1NT	2♣	♠ J9542
♡ 84	2♠	4♠	♡ A9765
◇ A963	P		◇ 54
♣ AQ8			♣ 3

East intends to crawl, but changes his mind. Once West bids 2♠, East's original five-count literally doubles in value. His fifth trump is worth a point, his doubleton diamond is also worth one, and his golden singleton adds another three.

The Stayman Family Tree

"Regular" Stayman
Responder bids 2♣ with at least one four-card major and eight points or more.

Garbage Stayman
Responder bids 2♣ with shortness in clubs and a weak hand.

Puppet Stayman
Responder bids 3♣ with one or more three-card majors and a game-going hand.

Crawling Stayman
Responder bids 2♣ with both majors and a weak hand.

It is possible to incorporate all four types of Stayman into your system because they are complementary. I do and it works beautifully.

Thank You, Mr. Jacoby

Jacoby Transfers

When opener bids 1NT:
  2♦ by responder promises at least five hearts.
  2♥ by responder promises at least five spades.

Any point count is possible.

      * * *

Opener is forced to bid partner's major.

Opener may jump with four trumps and a nice hand.

Take a look at some well-bid hands:

	Opener	*Responder*	
♠ 97	1NT	2♥*	♠ QJ654
♥ AKQ	2♠	2NT	♥ J82
♦ KJ73	P		♦ Q86
♣ QJ54			♣ K6

Responder embarked on an invitational path, which opener declined because of his very poor spade holding and indifferent hand. 3NT is a terrible contract that is well worth avoiding.

	Opener	*Responder*	
♠ A643	1NT	2♦*	♠ 5
♥ AQ76	3♥	4♥	♥ K8542
♦ 97	P		♦ Q10842
♣ AK5			♣ 98

Responder was intending to transfer and pass, but came to life once partner showed enthusiasm. Opener should strive to jump in responder's major with most hands that include four trumps.

	Opener	*Responder*	
♠ AQ7	1NT	2♣	♠ KJ865
♡ KQJ	2◊	3♠	♡ A742
◊ K73	4♠	P	◊ A106
♣ Q652			♣ 7

With five-four in the majors and a game-going hand, responder begins with Stayman rather than Jacoby. After the disappointing 2◊ rebid by opener, responder jumps in his five-card suit to force to game. (Advocates of Smolen would jump in hearts—the four-card suit—to insure that the stronger hand declares.)

	Opener	*Responder*	
♠ J4	1NT	2♡*	♠ Q109876
♡ AQ64	2♠	4♠	♡ K53
◊ A86	P		◊ 2
♣ A753			♣ K86

Responder showed good appreciation of his proven honors, spade texture and singleton diamond by bidding game. An invitational approach would have resulted in the partnership languishing in a part score. (For those pairs who use Texas transfers, a jump to 4♡ would be responder's first bid.)

	Opener	*Responder*	
♠ A9	2NT	3♡*	♠ 876542
♡ A654	3♠	P	♡ 72
◊ AK10			◊ 62
♣ KQJ7			♣ 842

Responder's hand was not very impressive, but he realized the necessity of escaping from notrump. Without transfers, he could never have ended up in 3♠.

		Opener	*Responder*		
♠	KQ7	1NT	2♡*	♠	J8652
♡	A8654	2♠	2NT	♡	J
◇	A5	4♠	P	◇	K742
♣	K76			♣	A53

Opener started well by opening 1NT. Opening 1♡ and finding a rebid after a 1♠ response would not have been fun. Responder had enough to invite game and opener wasted no time accepting.

Our last example answers the frequently-asked question, "How does responder handle a weak hand with a long minor when playing Jacoby?"

		Opener	*Responder*		
♠	QJ4	1NT	3◇*	♠	K85
♡	AJ876	P		♡	5
◇	Q7			◇	J109643
♣	KQJ			♣	874

The 1NT opening got the pair off to a good start. This allowed responder to make diamonds the trump suit. No muss, no fuss; just an easy + 110. (The 3◇ bid is alertable because is it a signoff.)

Jacoby transfers are here to stay. This very popular convention has eased and improved notrump bidding all over the world. There is no question that the bridge world owes a very big debt of gratitude to one of the legendary bridge pioneers, Mr. Oswald Jacoby.

CHAPTER 7
Exploding Popular Misconceptions

3NT—Not Always a Shutout Bid

One of the first auctions that beginners learn is: 1NT-3NT. The teacher explains that the 3NT response must end the bidding because if responder had been interested in slam, he would not have bid 3NT.

Unfortunately, a little knowledge is a dangerous thing. Some players believe that all 3NT bids have the effect of closing the bidding. This is absolutely not true! There are many times when a player should not pass partner's natural 3NT bid. Here are a few examples:

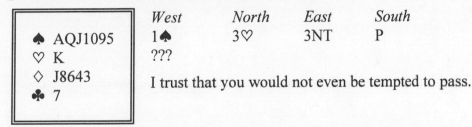

	West	North	East	South
♠ AQJ1095	1♠	3♡	3NT	P
♡ K	???			
◇ J8643				
♣ 7				

I trust that you would not even be tempted to pass.

There is absolutely nothing about your hand that suggests notrump. Partner's 3NT bid says that he believes the partnership has enough values for game. In addition, responder has at least one heart stopper and is unable to support spades. Partner did not say that he is sure that 3NT is the best contract. His bid was a suggestion, made under duress after the disruptive three-level preempt. He is not telling you to pass, he is doing the best he can.

If you were tempted to bid diamonds, take another look at your magnificent major suit, then bid 4♠.

What about noncompetitive auctions?

	You	Partner
♠ KJ104	1♣	1♠
♡ 8	2♣	3NT
◇ 743	???	
♣ AK865		

Bid 4♠. My opinion of pass cannot be expressed in mixed company. Partner has a balanced hand with four spades. He is suggesting an alternate contract. Your singleton heart is an asset in 4♠ but a liability in 3NT.

It would, however, be correct to pass 3NT with either of these hands:

♠ 9642   ♡ K105   ◇ KQ7   ♣ KQJ

♠ Q103   ♡ QJ74   ◇ K   ♣ KQ984

The first hand is flat as a pancake and includes terrible trumps. The second hand has only three spades, not enough to correct to 4♠.

On other auctions, responder might be the player making the final decision. Here is an example of a hand where responder should not pass opener's jump to 3NT.

	You	Partner
♠ J106	—	1♠
♡ A87543	2♡	3NT
◇ 3	???	
♣ AQ7		

Your 2♡ bid is correct because your good hand allows you the luxury of investigating hearts as well as spades. What does partner's 3NT bid promise? Although his exact point count might depend upon whom you ask, partner should have a strong balanced hand with exactly two hearts.

It would be crazy to pass 3NT with those cards. Which major should you bid? I would bid 4♠. Partner's spades rate to be better than your modest hearts. Had your hand been:

♠ 986   ♡ KQJ1065   ◇ AJ7   ♣ 2

you would make the obvious 4♡ rebid.

Pass 3NT with such lovely distribution—as well as fits in both majors? Bah humbug!

A Major Misconception

Opener must have four-card support to raise a one-of-a-major response.

Oh really? Please tell me what you would rebid with this hand.

	West	North	East	South
♠ KQ5	1◇	P	1♠	P
♡ AQ74	???			
◇ J8532				
♣ 3				

You cannot rebid your diamonds! You cannot bid notrump with a singleton club or reverse into hearts without a much stronger hand. You must raise to 2♠.

Would anything be different after a 1♣ opening?

	West	North	East	South
♠ A62	1♣	P	1♠	P
♡ AKJ7	???			
◇ 4				
♣ 96432				

Definitely not. Once again, the bid is 2♠.

What if opener has weak spades? Can he avoid the problem?

	West	North	East	South
♠ 432	1♣	P	1♠	P
♡ AKQJ	???			
◇ 7				
♣ Q7542				

Sorry, the answer is still **no**. I would hate to rebid 2♣ with these clubs. Bid 2♠.

Is anything different after a 1♡ response? Not really.

	West	North	East	South
♠ 5	1♣	P	1♡	P
♡ AQ6	???			
◇ 9874				
♣ AQ742				

Raise to 2♡. If you rebid 2♣ with this hand, you will not feel too well when partner is forced to pass holding:

♠ A984   ♡ K10975   ◇ 1062   ♣ 5

What would you do here?

West	North	East	South
1◇	P	1♡	P
???			

♠ 5
♡ 1096
◇ AKJ43
♣ AK76

Rebid 2♣, no problem.

♠ 6
♡ AQ7
◇ AQ742
♣ 6542

Although many would rebid 2♣, I am delighted to raise partner's 1♡ response to 2♡.

The power of opener's three-card major-suit raise is illustrated very well on the following deal. It was played in a team match in a national championship many years ago.

```
                    North
                    ♠ A109
                    ♡ A87
                    ◇ AJ7543
                    ♣ 6
    West                            East
    ♠ J87                           ♠ Q6
    ♡ KQJ9                          ♡ 106432
    ◇ Q10                           ◇ K982
    ♣ Q1094                         ♣ KJ
                    South
                    ♠ K5432
                    ♡ 5
                    ◇ 6
                    ♣ A87532
```

At both tables, North opened 1◇ and South responded 1♠. The similarity in the auctions ended there. At one table, North rebid his six-card diamond suit. South did not enjoy passing, but he could hardly bid again with his misfit and seven HCP. After a heart lead, declarer scored up his 2◇ contract by trumping one heart in dummy for + 90.

At the other table, North liked his spade support well enough to offer his partner an immediate raise. This made all the difference. Having located a major-suit fit and with great shape, South lost no time bidding 4♠.

Dummy's three trumps were a disappointment, but South demonstrated how good players operate. He won the heart lead with the ace and went to work on his clubs. He led a club to his ace and ruffed a club. He now cashed the ace and king of spades. Once both opponents followed, South was home free. He led another club from his hand, and although the suit did not divide three-three, he could not be stopped from developing his long suit. He lost two clubs and the ♠J and scored up a big gain for his team.

Food for thought? I certainly hope so. Opener has four cards when he raises responder's major, except when he has only three.

Supporting Opener's Minor Suit

For this not-so-dirty dozen, you are always East. What would you bid?

West	North	East	South
1◇	P	???	

♠ 643 ♡ 7 ◇ A643 ♣ Q9754

♠ A4 ♡ 98 ◇ 10765 ♣ K8643

♠ A ♡ 965 ◇ 8543 ♣ QJ432

♠ 543 ♡ — ◇ AQ85 ♣ 986532

Raise to 2◇ with all of these. No other action, including pass, would occur to me.

West	North	East	South
1♣	1♠	???	

♠ 42 ♡ 76 ◇ AQ854 ♣ J943

♠ 53 ♡ 854 ◇ Q843 ♣ AQ63

♠ 9754 ♡ 5 ◇ AK94 ♣ 5432

♠ 9 ♡ 742 ◇ A9765 ♣ K987

Once again, what is the problem? Bid 2♣ on all four.

West	North	East	South
1◇	2♡	???	

♠ 52 ♡ 87 ◇ K754 ♣ AQ873

♠ AQ ♡ 7 ◇ Q965 ♣ J76543

Bid 3◇. Two more no-brainers.

West	North	East	South
1♣	2♠	???	

♠ 854   ♡ A   ◇ J9754   ♣ KJ98

♠ 76   ♡ 74   ◇ AJ943   ♣ AJ43

Of course you bid 3 ♣. I can just hear your thoughts. "Marty, I don't mind some easy questions now and then, but I'm becoming bored. What's your point?"

Four auctions, 12 hands. What do they have in common? You are raising opener's minor with only four-card support.

Do you believe that this is a big deal? I certainly do not. However, I know first hand that many players believe that it is. They are under the impression, or were taught, that responder should only raise opener's minor suit opening with five-card support. Once and for all, I hope we have put that one to rest.

*   *   *

Speaking of teaching, years ago I had a long-time student who was hopelessly confused. I felt very badly and was determined to find **something** that the student could get right so that I could congratulate him.

I devoted two entire lessons to leading high from a doubleton! I then set up a deal where his partner opened 1♡ and my student would be on lead. I carefully arranged the ♡98 as the doubleton, as a "safety play."

I positioned myself nearby, ready to enjoy the finest moment of my teaching career. My student was evidently deep in thought. He then smiled and triumphantly led...the ♡8!

"Excuse me," I said, with superhuman restraint. "Do you remember me saying that you must lead top of a doubleton, so that your partner will know you can trump the third round of the suit?"

"I thought about that, Marty, but just last week you taught us *eight ever, nine never*"!!!

"Only Overcall With a Strong Suit" Oh Yeah?

Your RHO opens 1♣. Both sides are vulnerable. It is now your call.

♠ Q8543   ♡ 4   ◊ AK93   ♣ K43

♠ A   ♡ 86532   ◊ AKQ   ♣ 9764

♠ 98654   ♡ AK   ◊ J7543   ♣ A

♠ A5   ♡ J9764   ◊ AQ   ♣ Q965

Your RHO opens 2◊ weak. Neither side is vulnerable. What now?

♠ K7652   ♡ J   ◊ A5   ♣ A9653

♠ A9765   ♡ A4   ◊ 62   ♣ AQ63

♠ A6   ♡ K7532   ◊ 8654   ♣ AK

♠ A   ♡ Q8653   ◊ A63   ♣ AQ92

I do not know about you, but on every hand I would have overcalled in my lousy five-card major. Would I have liked a better suit? Of course (although if a bridge genie is going to honor a wish for me, I can do a lot better than ask for an extra honor). Perhaps I lack imagination, but I cannot imagine any alternative.

Yes, we like our long suits to have honors galore, but we cannot wait for perfect situations. We must play the hands we are dealt.

Who Should Declare? Who Cares!

Here are four bridge problems that I would like you to answer. Where am I heading? Do not concern yourself with that for now, my point will become clear enough in time.

	West	North	You	South
♠ 8 ♡ QJ10754 ♢ QJ52 ♣ 86	1♠ 3NT Bid 4♡.	P P	1NT ???	P

	West	North	You	South
♠ K ♡ KQJ9754 ♢ Q652 ♣ 9	1♣ 1♠ Bid 4♡.	P P	1♡ ???	P

	West	North	You	South
♠ QJ82 ♡ 6 ♢ 754 ♣ KJ965	1♡ 3♢ Bid 3NT.	P P	1♠ ???	P

	West	North	You	South
♠ A82 ♡ 75 ♢ AK965 ♣ A87	3♠ Bid 4♠.	P	???	

What **was** the method to my madness? The answers were trivially simple, so what's up? In each of those four hands, the player about to declare is the weaker hand (the player with the least high cards).

Did that cross your mind for even one second? Now that I brought it to your attention, are you bothered by it? Would you like to reconsider any of your actions?

I hope and assume that your answer to these very hypothetical questions were **no**. We cannot concern ourselves about which player is going to declare—we merely want to arrive at the best contract. Bridge is difficult enough without introducing additional variables.

I cannot tell you how many times in my life as a bridge teacher I have heard or been told: "It is bad to have the weak hand declare." This is just another popular misconception. The reality is: allowing the weaker hand to declare is slightly imperfect, it is **not** a problem.

In case you are not convinced, let us continue with a little Q & A.

Question: Isn't it *nice* to have the strong hand declare?

Answer: Sure. That is the main reason most players use conventions such as the Jacoby transfer, which allows the notrump bidder to declare most hands after opening 1NT or 2NT.

Question: How did this "strong hand must declare" idea ever get started?

Answer: It is preferable to have the stronger hand concealed from the enemy. In addition, "last is best." What this means is: we prefer that the better hand play fourth (last) when the opening lead is made, rather than second.

Question: Do experts worry about which player declares?

Answer: We certainly do not waste time or energy thinking about which player has more HCP. However, opening lead considerations are important to us. For example, with both sides vulnerable, you hold:

	West	North	You	South
♠ KJ3	2♠	3♡	P	???
♡ A94				
◊ K87				
♣ J976				

The expert mindset is: "I must avoid a spade lead through my KJ3."

"As much as I love to support partner's major, I need to declare and protect my spade holding. I must bid 3NT."

Here is the entire deal:

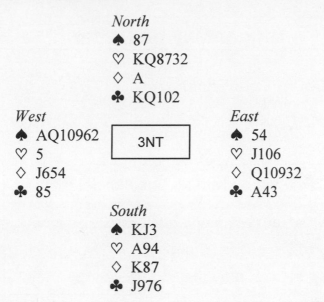

North
- ♠ 87
- ♡ KQ8732
- ◇ A
- ♣ KQ102

West
- ♠ AQ10962
- ♡ 5
- ◇ J654
- ♣ 85

3NT

East
- ♠ 54
- ♡ J106
- ◇ Q10932
- ♣ A43

South
- ♠ KJ3
- ♡ A94
- ◇ K87
- ♣ J976

Notice that 3NT by South is cold, even if West is allowed to see all the other cards. A spade lead will limit South to nine tricks; otherwise, he has time to make an overtrick by developing clubs. However, with North as declarer, 4♡ has no play after the obvious spade lead. Once West plays three rounds of spades, he succeeds in promoting a trump trick for East (the aesthetic uppercut). The ♣A is the setting trick.

Grist for the mill? For sure. But on most hands, I just apply K.I.S.S. (keep it simple, stupid). Do not give a second thought to declarer's name, gender, masterpoint holding or HCP. Just bid what you think you can make, and then root for your side to bring the contract home.

CHAPTER 8
Bigger May be Better

Open 2♣—Count Your Tricks

Let us take a look at how to handle really big hands—unbalanced ones in particular.

2♣ Opening with an Unbalanced Hand

Have at least as many quick tricks as losers,

and

Have at least nine playing tricks.

To review, **quick tricks** (also known as defensive tricks) refer to the number of tricks you would take on defense against an opponent's suit contract. Here is the complete list:

AK = 2; AQ = 1½; A = 1; KQ = 1; Kx = ½

Note that no suit can have more than two quick tricks and that jacks are never "quick."

Playing tricks refers to the number of tricks you would take as declarer playing in your long suit. Subtract your number of losers from 13.

Here is some important advice to round out your decision-making process. Always open 2♣ with six or more quick tricks, and **if you have a close decision, open 2♣.**

Use these guidelines to decide what to open with each of the hands on the next page.

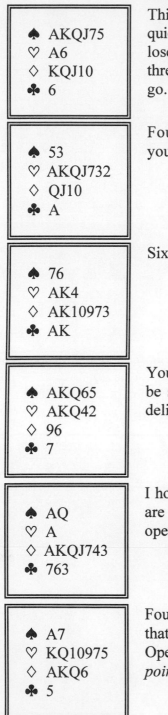

♠ AKQJ75
♡ A6
◇ KQJ10
♣ 6

This hand has four quick tricks and three losers. The quick tricks are the ♠ AK, ♡ A and ◇ KQ. The three losers are a heart, a diamond and a club. Hands with three losers must have ten playing tricks. All signs are go. Open 2♣.

♠ 53
♡ AKQJ732
◇ QJ10
♣ A

Four losers but only three quick tricks. Content yourself with 1♡.

♠ 76
♡ AK4
◇ AK10973
♣ AK

Six quick tricks. When so blessed, always open 2♣.

♠ AKQ65
♡ AKQ42
◇ 96
♣ 7

You have four quick tricks and three losers. It would be silly to open 1♠ and risk playing there, so be delighted to open 2♣.

♠ AQ
♡ A
◇ AKQJ743
♣ 763

I hope you would not hesitate with this beauty. You are likely to make 3NT opposite a Yarborough, so open 2♣.

♠ A7
♡ KQ10975
◇ AKQ6
♣ 5

Four quick tricks and four losers. It pays to assume that you will not lose any tricks with AKQ6 in a suit. Open 2♣. Only 18 HCP you say. I say (guess what), *points schmoints*.

2♣ and Beyond

Most players do not open 2♣ often enough with unbalanced hands that have less than a gazillion points. Even experts are guilty of this.

What about responding to 2♣? There are many schools of thought here: 2◇ negative, step responses, 2◇ waiting, even 2◇ positive.

Because most players use 2◇ as a waiting bid, I am going to proceed on that basis. Opener has the stronger hand; therefore, responder should usually be willing to allow the 2♣ opener to "speak" first. The only exception occurs when responder has a great suit that he is just dying to talk about.

Here are some examples (bids with asterisks are alertable):

		West	East		
♠	AQJ76	2♣	2◇	♠	83
♡	AKJ52	2♠	3♣*	♡	Q843
◇	A8	3♡	4♡	◇	97432
♣	7	P		♣	83

With only 19 HCP, many players would not open 2♣. I could not disagree more. How would you feel if you opened 1♠ and everyone passed? The answer to that question is far more relevant than "You can only open 2♣ with (pick your favorite number) HCP."

East does not have much, but the 2◇ response is painless. He must not pass 2♠, but needs to inform opener that his hand is very weak. The 3♣ second negative shows less than four HCP. Opener now shows his second suit via 3♡, which is forcing. When East makes the obvious raise to 4♡, all is well.

		West	East		
♠	AQ107	2♣	2◇	♠	K
♡	KQ	2NT	3◇*	♡	J108432
◇	AKQ6	3♡	4♡	◇	732
♣	QJ7	P		♣	853

The 2♣ opening followed by 2NT promises a hand slightly too strong for a 2NT opening. East can now utilize the same conventions he would have if West had opened 2NT. With his six-card suit, he is delighted to transfer to hearts and then raise to game.

	West	East	
♠ K	2♣	2♠	♠ AQJ107
♡ AKQ954	3♡	4♡	♡ J76
◇ AK843	4NT	5◇	◇ 72
♣ 7	6♡	P	♣ 842

With a good suit and values, East does not need to "wait" with 2◇. Once hearts becomes the agreed trump suit, it is easy for West to bid Blackwood and reach the excellent small slam.

	West	East	
♠ AQ73	2♣	2◇	♠ KJ8
♡ KQ7	3NT	6NT	♡ A83
◇ AKQ	P		◇ 8432
♣ KQJ			♣ 752

With 26 HCP, some would open 3NT, while others prefer to open 2♣ and rebid 3NT. Regardless, West shows a very strong balanced hand with the 3NT bid.

With eight HCP, East's interest was piqued as soon as partner opened 2♣. However, he had no reason to do anything other than wait. Once he learned that West had 25-27 HCP, only elementary arithmetic was required to bid 6NT.

	West	East	
♠ A84	2♣	3♣	♠ 952
♡ A	4NT	5◇	♡ K2
◇ AKQJ106	7NT	P	◇ 83
♣ KQ7			♣ AJ10962

The easiest of the bunch. Once East shows a good suit and sign of life with his 3♣ response, West could even show off and immediately jump to 7NT. Why don't I ever get these hands?

	West	East	
♠ KQJ10842	2♣	2◇	♠ 7
♡ AK	2♠	3♣*	♡ 8532
◇ A94	3♠	P	◇ 7532
♣ 6			♣ 8543

Only 17 HCP in West's hand, how low can we go? We are not actually low at all. With spades as trump, West has only four losers. Because these are offset by his four quick tricks, he is correct to open 2♣. It would be a crime to open 1♠ and have everyone pass because all partner had was the ◇K.

East seized the opportunity at his second turn with his very descriptive denial bid of 3♣. If ever anyone had a lousy hand, here it is. West's 3♠ bid is not forcing, and East is in a big hurry to end the auction. If West had more, he would have jumped to 4♠ or made a forcing bid in a new suit. This hand illustrates how you can stop short of game after opeing 2♣.

Auctions featuring big hands have an electric quality to them, especially when slam prospects are lively. As always, good partnership communication is essential.

The Truth About Reverses

No topic causes as much anxiety as the reverse. It may not be anyone's favorite, but it cannot be ignored. There is nothing wrong with hoping/ praying that reverses do not occur, but all players need a basic understanding of the concept. Besides, what is so bad about having a good hand?

Question: Why didn't you write about reverses in *Points Schmoints!*?

Answer: I was trying to avoid this very complex topic. However, after receiving so many questions about the reverse in the last few years, I felt that my students deserved an answer.

Question: How strong a hand does opener need to reverse?

Answer: With five-four distribution, opener should have at least 17 HCP. With six-four or six-five, he can have less. Here are examples of minimum, but acceptable, reverses.

West	North	East	South
1♣	P	1♠	P
2♡			

♠ K6   ♡ AQ76   ◇ 85   ♣ AKJ65

♠ 8   ♡ K953   ◇ K5   ♣ AKQ874

♠ 7   ♡ AK732   ◇ 8   ♣ AQ10965

Question: What about five-five distribution?

Answer: Never reverse with five-five. **A reverse guarantees that your first-bid suit is longer than your second**.

Question: Can opener reverse at the one level?

Answer: No, one-level bidding is just up the line.

Question: How can I recognize opener's reverse?

Answer: He must have bid a new suit at the two level—without jumping— which was higher ranking than the suit he bid first.

Question: Does opener promise a rebid after his reverse?

Answer: Absolutely, unless responder has jumped to game himself.

Question: If responder has bid at the two level, does anything change?

Answer: Yes. Opener does not need as big a hand to reverse.

Question: Are reverses still on in competition?

Answer: Yes. The 2♡ bid in the following auction still shows a big hand:

West	North	East	South
1◇	P	1♠	2♣
2♡			

Question: Are reverses forcing to game?

Answer: No, but they are forcing for one round.

Question: Can you give me an example of a good reverse auction?

Answer: Here you go.

		North	South	
♠ 4		1◇	1♠	♠ AJ6532
♡ AK105		2♡	2♠	♡ 82
◇ AKJ963		3◇	3NT	◇ Q4
♣ 98		P		♣ K75

North had only 15 HCP, but look at those two beautiful suits. That is a promotable hand if ever I saw one.

After North's reverse, South knew that his side had the values for game. However, he was in no hurry because opener had to take another bid. South used excellent judgement with his economical 2♠ bid. Had he bid 3♠, North would have been forced to bid 4◇ and miss the cold notrump game. This was a well-judged auction by both players.

The full deal:

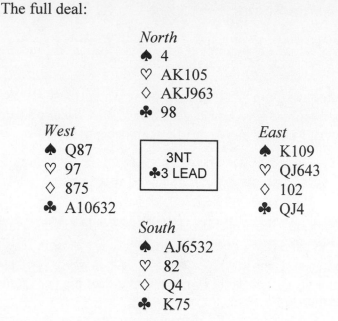

North
♠ 4
♡ AK105
◇ AKJ963
♣ 98

West
♠ Q87
♡ 97
◇ 875
♣ A10632

3NT
♣3 LEAD

East
♠ K109
♡ QJ643
◇ 102
♣ QJ4

South
♠ AJ6532
♡ 82
◇ Q4
♣ K75

After winning the opening club lead, South had no trouble taking ten tricks. No other game would have made.

Question: What else should I know about reverses?

Answer: Auctions that are forcing for one round, but not necessarily game forcing, are tricky. Even experts sometimes find themselves on shaky ground after a reverse. Opening 2NT with...

♠ AQ ♡ KQJ5 ◇ KJ765 ♣ KJ

...to avoid a reverse auction after 1◇ by you, 1♠ by partner, definitely does not make you a coward in my book.

Slam Bidding Made Easier

Do you believe that the most effective way to get to slam is to race to bid Blackwood? No way!

One key to effective slam bidding is to know when to use Blackwood and what to do when it is not appropriate. As Easley Blackwood was the first to admit, Blackwood is not the answer to all slam decisions.

The sole function of Blackwood is to discover partner's number of aces. On many hands, though, quantity is not the answer; what we seek is location, location, location.

The two best reasons to forego Blackwood are: you have a void or a worthless suit. Let us take these one at a time. If you are void in a suit and partner's ace is in that suit, his ace is "wasted." In other words, you already had the suit under control. You would rather partner had his ace in another suit where you did have a loser.

A worthless suit, one with no ace or king, for instance, needs help. If your Blackwood inquiry reveals that you are missing an ace, you still will not know if partner can help your weak suit. If he cannot, you will be down in your slam before you know it.

Now take a look at some slam hands. Although Roman Keycard Blackwood (RKC) is all the rage, and does have certain advantages, we will use old-fashioned Blackwood. To refresh your memory (especially for RKC advocates), responses to 4NT are: zero or four aces, bid 5♣; one ace, 5♦; two aces 5♥, three aces 5♠.

	West	East	
♠ AQ54	1♡	1♠	♠ KJ8732
♡ AQJ75	3♠	4♣	♡ K2
◇ 4	4◇	4NT	◇ 985
♣ Q95	5♡	6♠	♣ A3

The first three bids were routine. East was interested in slam after 3♠, but avoided 4NT because of his diamond weakness. If opener held the major-suit aces, East would still be at the mercy of partner's diamond holding.

East's 4♣ cuebid showed a club control, promising a holding that prevented the opponents from taking the first two tricks in that suit. West now reciprocated in diamonds. Just what the doctor ordered. It was now child's play for East to Blackwood into slam. Notice that we were able to cuebid and Blackwood on the same hand. Very nice, we really got our money's worth.

Now for an easy one.

	West	East	
♠ KQ2	1◇	1♡	♠ 5
♡ A9	3◇	4NT	♡ KQ854
◇ AQJ852	5♡	6◇	◇ K643
♣ 83	P		♣ A74

I never said that perfect Blackwood hands had become extinct. With controls in every suit, East was interested only in opener's aces. The 6◇ contract was as easy to make as it was to bid.

		West	East		
♠	AQ2	1♡	2♠	♠	KJ1076
♡	AKJ7543	3♡	4♡	♡	Q106
◇	—	4♠	5♣	◇	KJ
♣	865	7♡	P	♣	AK3

I like East's jump shift to 2♠. When he then raises to 4♡, he gives a good description of a hand with five or six nice spades and interest in a heart slam. West has a beautiful hand, but knows that bidding Blackwood with a void is a no-no. He cuebids 4♠ and hopes for the best. This bid promises first-round control of spades because it is made beyond the level of game. East's 5♣ cuebid also promises the ace of that suit. This is all West needs. Knowing that spades will run, he confidently bids the grand.

		West	East		
♠	9	1♡	4◇*	♠	AQ3
♡	AK10653	4NT	5♡	♡	Q987
◇	9754	6♡	P	◇	6
♣	KQ			♣	A7532

The key here was East's 4◇ splinter bid. When playing this convention, East's majestic double jump promised an opening bid with four-card heart support and a void or singleton in diamonds. Knowing that diamonds were under control, West needed no further encouragement.

		West	East		
♠	KQ2	1NT	4NT	♠	A103
♡	K76	5◇	6◇	♡	A7
◇	K10953	P		◇	A874
♣	A2			♣	K1093

After West's obvious 1NT opening, East evaluated well by upgrading his 15 HCP. He loved his prime cards and two tens and correctly invited slam with 4NT. The bridge term for this bid is "quantitative."

Some players sitting West would have declined the invitation with only 15 HCP, but this West was made of sterner stuff. He appreciated that his nice five-card suit increased the value of this hand. A second look at his prime cards encouraged him to bid on. However, West did not just close his eyes and accept the invitation by bidding 6NT. He bid 5◇ to show his suit (note that 5◇ was not meant to show his one ace) and awaited developments.

The rest was easy. With his nice diamond support, East was delighted to raise to 6◇. Although a trump trick had to be lost, 6◇ made easily by ruffing a heart. 6NT was a reasonable contract, but it was doomed. Three spades, two hearts, four diamonds and two club tricks just do not add to 12.

Why was 6◇ laydown with two balanced hands and only 30 HCP? A Bergenism applies here which can prove to be a nice evaluating tool, especially for slam. "It is uncanny how well hands work out when they have very few (if any) jacks." I am not saying that I would rather have a two than a jack, but because jacks are the most overrated of honors, it bothers me to count them as a full point.

	West	East	
♠ KQ7432	1♠	2♣	♠ AJ10
♡ KJ106	2♡	3♠	♡ AQ5
◇ Q6	4♣	4♡	◇ 93
♣ A	4♠	P	♣ KJ854

The first three bids are quite logical, West applying the "six-four-six" principle. East's jump to 3♠ promised at least an opening bid with spade support. (If playing two-over-one game forcing, the jump shows extra values).

West was very interested in slam, but concerned about his diamonds. He cuebid 4♣, hoping to hear a 4◇ bid from East. East's 4♡ bid said a mouthful. Because **controls are cuebid up the line**, East's 4♡ bid not only promised a heart control, but it denied a diamond control.

West was disappointed, but nothing plus nothing equals nothing. No diamond control, no slam. Notice that by embarking on a cuebidding sequence, both players were involved in the decision-making process.

I hope that you were not too frustrated by this comparatively tame hand. After five beautifully-bid laydown slams, I thought a dose of reality was in order. Slam on every hand is just too much.

CHAPTER 9
Women I Have Known

Enthusiastic Amateur Wears Glass Slipper

One of the great human interest stories in the world of big-time bridge involved a 62-year old grandmother from Scarsdale, NY. When I met Luella Slaner in 1978, she had just begun playing duplicate, although she had been playing bridge for years. She played on two country club teams during the summer, besides some "bridge with the girls."

Luella became my student. For the next few years we would play duplicate together, mostly in local club games. Occasionally she would attend a tournament, but other commitments prevented her from doing much traveling. She had accumulated 111 masterpoints by the end of 1981.

"I have free time in March, Marty. Are there any tournaments nearby?"

"Now that you mention it, the Spring Nationals will take place in late March in Niagara Falls."

"That sounds good, what would we play in?"

"My favorite event is the Vanderbilt Knockout Teams. You play until you are knocked out—similar to a tennis tournament. It's the premier event of the Spring Nationals."

"Premier event, I'm not good enough for that! All the experts will be playing. What would we do after being knocked out? I don't want to fly to Niagara Falls for just one day of bridge."

"No problem. Every day there are many other events we can play in. Besides, competing in a national tournament is a great experience, something that every duplicate player should try at least once. As for playing against experts, wouldn't you love to play a round of golf with Jack Nicklaus? One unique feature of bridge is that it presents an opportunity for the average player to compete against a world champion."

"I see what you mean. Maybe we can play against Omar Sharif. Will he be there? That would make the trip worthwhile."

"He might be. He sometimes attends these."

"Marty, you called it the Vanderbilt Teams. What does that mean?"

"We would recruit teammates, so that our two pairs are playing simultaneously. Let's refer to our team as the good guys, while our opponents are the bad guys. You and I will sit North-South and play hands 1-8 against two bad guys. Meanwhile our teammates will sit East-West against a second pair of bad guys. They will start with boards 9-16. After each table finishes their eight hands, they will summon a caddy to exchange the boards. We will then play 9-16 and the other table will play 1-8. When we have each finished playing the 16 boards (one quarter of the match), we will compare results and determine a score. Each day we will play 64 boards against one new team. The overall winner will advance, the loser will look for a new event."

"Sounds like fun. But 64 hands in one day! I've never done that before. I'm not sure that I'm up to it."

"No problem. Each player is only required to play 32 boards. We'll have five players, so you'll play the first half and can then relax."

"That's a relief. Still, we would need some great teammates to help us. Who would you get?"

And the rest, as they say, is history. Let me quote from *The New York Times*, Sunday April 4, 1982. I just happen to have a copy handy. Alan Truscott wrote:

A Cinderella Story

"In the traditional fairy tale, Cinderella had six remarkable hours that ended, or almost ended, at midnight. In a variation on the Cinderella tale, one that took place at the Spring Nationals last month, the time of glory lasted six full days, again ending, or almost ending, at midnight.

"In this case, Cinderella was not a teenaged girl who was not expected at the ball. Instead, she was a 62-year old grandmother who was not expected to make a mark in the Vanderbilt Team championship, and, indeed, had never before competed in a major national event.

"Cinderella's name was Luella Slaner, a woman of many talents: expert golfer, former mayor of her hometown Scarsdale, and an expert on fusion energy, which will utilize the limitless resources of the oceans. But at the bridge table, as she would be the first to admit, she is an enthusiastic amateur rather than an expert.

"Playing the role of Fairy Godmother was Marty Bergen of White Plains, who encouraged Mrs. Slaner to venture into tournament play. He recruited three spirited "horses": Warren Rosner of Nanuet, NY, Mark Cohen of New York City, and Jerry Goldfein of Chicago, all of whom presumably began life as little white mice.

"The coach rolled along smoothly, and the horses were strong. They raced past a string of teams that included bunches of world champions and national champions. On the fifth day, in the semi-final, they trailed by 36 points against substantially the same team that won the 1981 Spingold. But the horses pulled strongly, and the match was won by five points.

"Cinderella was now in the final, only the second woman to reach that point in a decade. And for a time it seemed that she might even win the title. After she had played her quota of 32 deals, the scores were exactly tied. But in the evening session the opponents were powerful and efficient. The horses were tired, and at midnight they turned back into white mice.

"The glass slipper will arrive for Cinderella next November. By a quirk of the regulations, her second-place finish has earned her team a place in the team trials that will determine the 1983 North American team for the World Championship."

P.S. We did not win the team trials, but it was a wonderful experience for Cinderella and her entourage.

P.P.S. Luella's second major national event was the 1983 Spingold Master Knockout Teams. Once again, I would like to quote from *The New York Times*.

Another Cinderella Victory for Luella Slaner's Team

"NEW ORLEANS, July 24—The Cinderella team of 1982 did it again here Saturday night in the American Contract Bridge League's Summer Nationals. The New York group headed by Luella Slaner of Scarsdale, which upset all predictions by reaching the Vanderbilt final in Niagara Falls, NY last year, reached the Spingold semifinal by snatching a last-deal victory from the top-seeded team.

"In the Vanderbilt, Mrs. Slaner lost in the final to Dr. George Rosenkranz. She had sweet revenge here against the same opponents, including three world champions. Actually, when we learned that we would oppose this most formidable team, Luella's reaction was, 'Good, we have a score to settle with them!'"

P.S. We won our semifinal match before again being defeated in the final. Although Cinderella never became a bride, in her two adventures as a bridesmaid, grandma had a blast as the belle of the ball.

The Ultimate Happy Ending

The following appeared in *The New York Times* on Monday, July 23, 1984, but definitely not in the bridge column.

"At 10:20 P.M. Saturday, July 21, 1984 an announcement was made at the Summer National tournament in Washington, D.C. that resulted in cheering, yelling and general pandemonium. 'Some of them cried, some of them laughed, and some of them smiled,' said Henry Francis, Editor of the American Contract Bridge League *Bulletin*. People who had been enemies for years smiled at each other."

What was it that could have caused the bridge world to react in this fashion? What could have occurred at a bridge tournament that garnered extensive front-page coverage all over the world?

I was a member of the third-seeded team led by Dr. George Rosenkranz. We had won our first two matches of the Spingold, a premier team event, handily. However, on Thursday evening (July 19), we had been involved in a close match against a tough West Coast team. Around midnight, after comparing scores, we learned that we had won by the very smallest of margins—always an exhilarating feeling. It was then that we heard the kind of terrible news that puts everything in perspective. Edith had been abducted at gunpoint!

Edith was Edith Rosenkranz, wife of our captain George Rosenkranz. With a doctorate in chemistry, he helped develop the first birth control pill. He was also the founder of Syntex Corporation and that Company's president at the time.

If that is not enough, George Rosenkranz is also Mexico's leading bridge player. As an authority on bidding theory, he has written many books and articles. Edith is also a fine player, and both have won many tournaments, besides representing Mexico in numerous World Championships. In addition, the Rosenkranzes are regarded as two of the nicest and most popular people in the bridge world.

We learned that Mrs. Rosenkranz had been kidnapped as she had been walking a friend to her car in the hotel garage. If the situation were not incredible enough, let me point out that the tournament was being held at the Sheraton Washington, a scant three miles from the White House.

The following day, Friday July 20th, was like nothing that I ever could have imagined. There were reporters everywhere, as well as swarms of photographers. People were saying that they had seen FBI agents. I was able to confirm this first hand, as our team was questioned by them that morning. We later learned that there were eighty to one hundred agents working on the case. No bridge players were discussing slams or leads, or the "scandal" of a few days before; they were speculating about guns, ransoms and motives. Armed police officers surrounded the hotel.

Obviously, Dr. Rosenkranz was not going to be playing any more bridge that week. In an unprecedented move, the ACBL ruled that he and his partner, Eddie Wold, could remain on our team, but would be exempt from the normal playing requirements. Those of us who did play were hounded by the press. In another unprecedented move, our Friday match was relocated to an obscure corner of the hotel, away from all the other competition. We managed to win another close match on a day where the intense concentration needed was not easy to come by.

Dr. Rosenkranz received a ransom note that day, reportedly for $1 million. Television stations and newspapers reported the story nonstop. Any willing bridge player was interviewed, especially if he knew the victim. There were rumors that the kidnapper(s) was a bridge player, not surprising given that there were some four thousand in attendance at the tournament.

Saturday we played our third consecutive close match. And then, with one quarter to go, came the announcement that we had all been praying for: Edith had been rescued and was alive and well and unharmed.

She had been kidnapped and held for ransom by a group of three men, led by a bridge player with financial problems. After picking up the ransom money, their van was followed and they were arrested and charged.

When we saw Mrs. Rosenkranz on Monday, she was amazingly composed. Incredibly, she was more concerned with the outcome of our matches than her own nightmare. What a trooper!

By the way, Larry Cohen, Jeff Meckstroth, Eric Rodwell and I succeeded in winning the Spingold for Edith and George.

Bridge hands and tournaments come and go. But I am quite confident that every participant in the 1984 Summer Nationals in Washington, DC will remember that tournament as long as he lives.

That's No Bridge Player, That's My Wife

One of the most interesting phenomena of bridge is the husband-wife partnership. Some would say "husbands and wives were not intended to play bridge together." Others would disagree. But everyone would agree that couples bridge has a potential that mere mortals cannot even contemplate.

Who could possibly predict the outcome when a couple plays bridge together? Who could know what took place at dinner before the game, at the party the preceding evening, or even in the car on the way over? Even if he did know, could he be farsighted enough to say what aberrations would result and what form they would take?

On the following hand from yesteryear, I was South. My partner was none other than the mother of my children, or as some would say, my ex-wife (in case you are curious, playing bridge together was not our problem). Could you have predicted the final contract?

North (Carole)
- ♠ —
- ♡ A76
- ◇ KJ109742
- ♣ K87

West
- ♠ K1043
- ♡ Q
- ◇ 8653
- ♣ Q963

> 4♡ Dbl
> ♣3 LEAD

East
- ♠ Q975
- ♡ K10842
- ◇ A
- ♣ 1054

South (Marty)
- ♠ AJ862
- ♡ J953
- ◇ Q
- ♣ AJ2

West	North	East	South
—	1◇	P	1♠
P	2◇	P	2♡
P	3♡!!	P	4♡
P	P	Dbl	all pass

The bidding proceeded normally until Carole's 3♡ bid. Her best action was to bid 3◇, which would have resulted in my bidding and making 3NT.

However it should be stated that my ex was always eager to avoid declaring (at least in bridge). East doubled firmly; rumor has it that his call was heard by several low-flying aircraft.

West's lead of the ♣3 rode to my jack. I wasted no time knocking out the ◇A, remembering: **"When in doubt, develop your side suit."** I won the club return with my ace and played a third round to dummy's king. A high diamond from dummy was ruffed by East's deuce and overruffed by my ♡3. I cashed the ♠A and ruffed a spade on the board. Another high diamond was greeted by East's ♡4 and my ♡5.

I ruffed a spade with dummy's ♡7 to continue with the fourth round of diamonds. East, whose face was rapidly turning beet red, tried ruffing with the ♡10. I overruffed with my jack for my ninth trick. Dummy's ♡A was still looking good as we scored up 4♡ doubled.

East and West now began a boisterous discussion of who should have done what. The last word (as always) was left to Carole. "Well played, Marty. Weren't those beautiful diamonds that I gave you? Any chance that you'll return the favor?"

*   *   *

Generation Gap

Back in 1994, I was very hopeful of getting a celebrity to endorse *Points Schmoints!* My first choice was Omar Sharif; a bridge celebrity as well as renowned actor. On the day that I received his glowing endorsement, I was on top of the world.

Later that day I received a phone call from Laurie, my daughter of 23 years. "Hi dad, how are you?"

"Great, honey, I couldn't be better. I just received the celebrity endorsement I was hoping for and he loved *Points Schmoints*! With Omar Sharif's statement on the front cover, I expect people to take special notice of the book."

"That's wonderful, dad. I'm really happy for you. I just have one question. Who is Omar Sharif?"

CHAPTER 10
Bidding More with Less

Problematic Preempts

The opening weak two-bid leads to many questions. Here are a few that I have received lately.

Dear Marty: I opened 2♢ holding four spades. My opponents acted as if I had stolen their dessert. Did I do something wrong?

M. G. in New York

Dear Falsely Accused: Not as far as I am concerned. With a hand like:

♠ J643   ♡ 3   ♢ KQ10954   ♣ 92

I would always preempt in diamonds. I cannot lose sleep about a possible spade fit. Pass? No way. Bridge is a bidder's game.

Dear Marty: I was all set to preempt 3♠ with...

♠ KJ108532   ♡ 42   ♢ 6   ♣ 753

...when my RHO opened 2♡. Unwilling to let them talk me out of my bid, I jumped to 3♠, as intended. My partner was very impressed. Am I ready for the big time?

P. F. in Chicago

Dear Jumpy: Do not quit your day job. One popular statement that applies is: "You can't preempt a preempt." Therefore, your jump showed strength, not weakness. Bidding 3♠ over 2♡ would be correct with:

♠ AK10943   ♡ 5   ♢ A64   ♣ KQ3

With your actual weak hand, you will have to pass for now.

Dear Marty: Playing in a recent duplicate, my partner opened 2♠ and I had the following:

♠ 6   ♡ KQ854   ◇ KQ93   ♣ AJ2

With my nice hand I knew that I had to bid. Some of my counterparts responded 3♡, others bid 2NT and a few brave souls jumped to 3NT. What would you have done?

S.K. confused, in Waco, TX

Dear Confused: When partner opens with a weak two-bid, picture a good suit and little or no outside strength. It is also realistic to presume that partner does not have length in your longest suit. Give partner:

♠ AQJ852   ♡ 9   ◇ 652   ♣ 1063

Where would you like to play opposite your hand?

Answer: a spade partscore. You should have passed. If anyone tries to tell you that you should respond to partner's preempt whenever you have an opening bid, as Dionne Warwick would say, just "walk on by."

*   *   *

Of course, bidding more with less does entail certain risks.

A fellow made a bad bid and went for 1400. "I'm sorry," he said to his partner, "I had a card misplaced." His partner innocently asked, "Only one?"

After Partner's Weak Two-Bid

What should you do after partner opens with a weak two-bid? How many points do you need to respond? I hope you are not fixated on the number 13. Once partner shows less than an opening bid, nothing could be less relevant.

If you also have a weak hand, the opponents can do very well if you allow them to exchange information. Unless you are playing against me, I recommend that you not be so obliging.

What is extremely relevant is your trump holding and The Law of Total Tricks (The LAW). When you have a fit, be eager to **support with support**. Sock it to them, and apply *points schmoints!*

Here are five hands for you to respond with after partner opens 2♡ and your RHO passes. Neither side is vulnerable.

Bid 4♡, what's the problem? Follow the LAW. You have four hearts and partner has six. With ten trumps, you belong at the four level.

I will attempt to ease the anxiety of those worriers and/or analytical souls who are concerned about jumping to game with only five HCP. I know that you are afraid to get doubled and go for a number.

It is unlikely that the final contract will be 4♡ doubled. The opponents have the balance of power and the master suit. It is dollars to donuts that they will bid. In fact there is an excellent chance that they can make a slam. You certainly have nothing to stop them.

♠ A84
♡ A75
◇ 8432
♣ 652

Bid 3♡. Opener has six trumps and you have three, so it is safe to compete to the three level.

♠ 84
♡ A83
◇ AK752
♣ A83

Uh oh, a good hand! Now you are forced to think. Even opposite a dead minimum such as...

♠ 972   ♡ QJ10654   ◇ 964   ♣ K

...you have excellent prospects for ten tricks. Bid 4♡.

Perhaps it says something about my personality, but I love the fact that you are making the same 4♡ bid with bad hands as well as good ones. Partner will not care, he is going nowhere. Meanwhile, you have put maximum pressure on the enemy, who will not enjoy trying to sort things out.

♠ AK65
♡ 84
◇ KQ74
♣ A83

Bid 2NT. Although this hand contains more HCP than the previous one, it is not as good because of the inferior trump fit. 2NT asks partner to tell you more about his hand. You will only bid game if he shows more than a minimum.

♠ KQ5
♡ —
◇ KQ732
♣ KQ432

Pass. *Points schmoints.* Even if partner has...

♠ A7   ♡ KQ9875   ◇ 86   ♣ 865

...where are you going? You cannot make 3NT. Your heart void is a **huge** liability. In my experience, even Life Masters fail this test at the table.

Surviving the Preempt

Preempts can cause trouble for the opponents. It is not easy to know when or how to compete when the enemy has deprived you of valuable bidding space. Here is some good general advice:

The player with shortness in the enemy's suit is the one who should strive to act after an opponent's preempt.

With neither side vulnerable, you are North and the auction proceeds:

West	North	East	South
3♡	???		

♠ 105
♡ A4
♢ AKQJ974
♣ 62

Bid 3NT. All you need from partner in order to make this is an ace. In fact, you might even be successful opposite as little as:

♠ K842 ♡ 83 ♢ 62 ♣ Q8754 ·

To make 5♢, you need three tricks from partner.

Yes, it would be nice to have stoppers in spades and/or clubs. However, **you can't worry about sneak attacks**.

♠ QJ6
♡ QJ
♢ KJ53
♣ KQJ4

Pass. You have 16 HCP and you should pass them all. This aceless mess is nothing more than a pile of garbage. You have a grand total of one and a half quick tricks.

♠ 86
♡ AQ
♢ KJ87
♣ AK1095

Overcall 3NT. The cheapest game is often the easiest game. This is especially true after an enemy preempt.

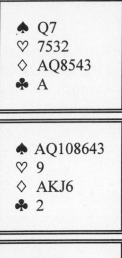

♠ Q7
♡ 7532
◇ AQ8543
♣ A

Pass. Your only alternative is to overcall 4◇. What are you planning to do with all your losing hearts? Partner never promised any diamond support. Stay out of this one for now. Be wary of bidding when you have length in the opponent's suit.

♠ AQ108643
♡ 9
◇ AKJ6
♣ 2

Bid 4♠. Needing so little from partner to make a game, you must not bid less. Because you cannot "preempt a preempt," your bid promises great strength. If partner has a few good cards, you have lively chances for slam.

♠ A
♡ KQ4
◇ KQ743
♣ A832

Bid 3NT. You may not like bidding this with a singleton, but you cannot afford to worry about such mundane matters. If you overcall 4◇ you will have two happy opponents.

♠ AQ96
♡ 9
◇ K854
♣ A1042

Double. While you would like to have more high cards to force partner to bid at this level, your singleton is worth its weight in gold. Do take notice of the three quick tricks.

♠ AK85
♡ 63
◇ AKQ74
♣ 93

Double. You are hoping that partner bids spades, notrump, diamonds or that he passes. If he bids 4♣, you are prepared to bid 4◇ and hope for the best.

West	*North*	*East*	*South*
3♡	???		

♠ AQJ985
♡ —
◇ 532
♣ K954

Bid 3♠. You do not have many HCP, but who cares with this shape and that great suit? Experience has shown that **hands with voids contain magical properties**. In fact, if the enemy had opened 4♡, you would close your eyes and bid 4♠.

♠ KJ762
♡ 7
◇ A8
♣ AKJ65

Cuebid 4♡. After the preempt, the Michaels cuebid promises a very good hand with spades and a minor. Partner will bid spades if possible; otherwise he will head for your minor.

♠ 9532
♡ AQ
◇ KQ10
♣ AQ98

Bid 3NT. It is not crazy to double, but with two heart stoppers try for the nine-trick game. If partner were to respond to your double with four of a minor, you would have arrived in no-man's land.

♠ KQJ102
♡ 6
◇ AJ863
♣ 87

Bid 3♠. You are not strong enough for a 4♡ cuebid. This hand is far too good for a pass; therefore make the economical 3♠ overcall.

Now when the opponents preempt, you will be poised and ready. When your shape is right, your results will be out of sight.

CHAPTER 11
Obeying The LAW

The Ten Commandments of The LAW

The LAW is based on these ten principles. Of course, continue to bid your major-suit games with 26 points and eight trumps.

1. You are *always* safe bidding to the level equal to your number of trumps. For example, with eight trumps, compete to the eight-trick (two-) level. Corollary: avoid bidding beyond your number of trumps.

2. Always try to define your trump length for partner.

3. Your trump length is far more important than distribution or HCP.

4. If the opponents have a fit and stop at the two level, balance to the three level with either eight or nine trumps.

5. You will rarely get a bad result when competing to the three level with nine trumps. However, the four level is sometimes too high even if you have a ten-card fit, especially with 5-3-3-2 distribution.

6. A singleton is nice to have, but in itself is not sufficient reason to violate The LAW. On the other hand, voids, freakish distribution or a two-suited hand are reasons to bid on, even if you are short a trump.

7. Particularly for tactical reasons, be eager to bid 4♠ over 4♡, even before the opponents get there.

8. Do not let vulnerability prevent you from following The LAW.

9. Major warning: beware of length in the opponent's suit. Your offensive potential is severely limited.

10. The LAW is not perfect. Occasionally you will get a bad result from using it. However, I guarantee that you will be a big winner in the long run. There is no doubt that it is more accurate for competitive bidding than the judgment of the best player in the world.

Do You Know The LAW?

Here are 20 opportunities to show your stuff. For all problems, both sides are vulnerable and you are East. Take five points for each correct answer. Good luck.

	West	North	East	South
♠ 9752 ♡ 864 ♢ 7 ♣ 97543	1♠	Dbl	???	

Bid 3♠. This is a perfect weak jump raise after the opponent's takeout double. If you were afraid because you were vulnerable, take some vitamins.

	West	North	East	South
♠ AJ43 ♡ Q7 ♢ Q109 ♣ K943	2♡	3♣	???	

Pass because you have only an eight-card fit. The LAW tells us that we will have a better chance to defeat 3♣ than to make a high-level heart contract.

	West	North	East	South
♠ A2 ♡ AJ87653 ♢ 3 ♣ Q104	— 2♡	— 3♢	1♡ ???	Dbl

Bid 4♡. Seven hearts plus partner's three means you have a ten-card fit. Isn't this an easy game?

	West	North	East	South
♠ QJ7543 ♡ A5 ♢ A63 ♣ 72	— 2♠	— 3♣	1♠ ???	2♣

Bid 3♠. You have a nine-card fit.

	West	North	East	South
♠ 87 ♡ 975 ♢ AQ6 ♣ 98643	3♡	P	???	

Bid 4♡. Seven plus three equals ten.

West	North	East	South
2♠	P	???	

♠ K53
♡ K83
◇ A74
♣ 8532

3♠ is your bid with nine trumps.

West	North	East	South
1♡	P	???	

♠ 92
♡ K9873
◇ 83
♣ 8632

Bid 4♡. Your partnership has a ten-card fit. Vulnerable, schmulnerable.

West	North	East	South
—	—	1♠	Dbl
2♠	4♡	???	

♠ K8632
♡ —
◇ KJ543
♣ AJ2

Pass with only an eight-card trump fit. An expert bid 4♠ here. He got doubled and went down 800 when 4♡ was not making.

Partner held:

♠ 1074   ♡ QJ96   ◇ 87   ♣ K943

West	North	East	South
1♠	P	P	2♣
2♡	3♣	???	

♠ J872
♡ 94
◇ 109732
♣ 64

If you were playing Bergen Raises, you would have bid 3♠ the first time. Do it now. With your nine-card fit, this is easy.

For your information, a national champion held this hand and passed throughout. His silence was compounded when opener's hand was...

♠ AKQ65   ♡ KQ63   ◇ 85   ♣ K3

...and both 3♣ and 3♠ were cold.

	West	North	East	South
♠ KJ532	—	—	1♠	2♣
♡ AJ6	2♠	3♣	???	
◇ J74				
♣ A8				

Pass. You have only eight trumps.

If a plus score is on your horizon, five tricks on defense are far more likely than nine on offense. Of course, if partner has a fourth trump, he will compete to 3♠.

	West	North	East	South
♠ 6432	1◇	Dbl	2◇	3♣
♡ K87	3◇	4♣	???	
◇ Q9432				
♣ 8				

Bid 4◇. Partner should have five diamonds to compete to 3◇ over 3♣. Your side has ten diamonds, hence the 4◇ bid. As for the 2◇ raise, I cannot award it an "A."

I do like the decision to ignore those emaciated spades after the double. However, I would have jumped to 3◇ to show a weak hand with good support. If you had, you would probably have bought the contract for 3◇.

	West	North	East	South
♠ K653	1♣	P	1♠	3◇
♡ KJ7	3♠	4◇	???	
◇ A64				
♣ 532				

Double. A famous world champion bid 4♠ and went down one when 4◇ was not making.

Having only eight trumps and 4-3-3-3 distribution along with the balance of power should have steered East to defend, not declare.

	West	North	East	South
♠ AK65	—	—	—	1♡
♡ 62	4♣	4♡	???	
◇ 8543				
♣ 743				

Bid 5♣. Partner should have eight clubs for his preempt, giving your side eleven of them.

	West	North	East	South
♠ J86532	—	1♦	1♠	Dbl
♡ A	2♣	4♡	???	
♦ 6532				
♣ A7				

Pass. The opponents probably have a four-four fit, leaving partner with four of their trumps.

They will not enjoy the bad split. With a tenth trump, you would bid 4♠ and not be concerned.

	West	North	East	South
♠ J965	—	—	—	1♠
♡ AJ10	2NT	4♠	???	
♦ K854				
♣ 87				

Pass. Too many players would bid 5♦ after partner's unusual notrump. You know better.

With only a nine-card diamond fit, the five level is too high. You should also be aware that your spades will be relevant only when that suit is trump. If partner has a freak hand such as...

♠ — ♡ 3 ♦ QJ9732 ♣ KQ10543

...he will bid again.

	West	North	East	South
♠ Q854	—	—	—	1♡
♡ 53	1♠	2♣	???	
♦ K72				
♣ 8632				

Bid 3♠. I recommend that you play weak jump raises after partner's overcall.

	West	North	East	South
♠ AKQJ6	—	—	1♠	Dbl
♡ KJ84	3♠	4♡	???	
♦ J3				
♣ K7				

Double. This is another hand from real life. The expert who held these cards bid 4♠ and played it well to go down one. However, 4♡ had no chance; the opponents would not have been able to cope with your trumps. Take half credit for passing—at least you went plus. It certainly is nice to use The LAW to outbid the experts.

	West	North	East	South
♠ A85	—	—	1NT	P
♡ A1076	2◇*	P	???	
◇ AK94				
♣ 84	* *2◇ is a transfer to 2♡.*			

Bid 3♡. This may have started off as a minimum 1NT opening, but what a lovely hand for a heart contract. Bidding 2♡ would be negligent. Partner's hand was:

♠ 62   ♡ K98542   ◇ 6   ♣ 9753.

Partner would be delighted to raise 3♡ to 4♡, but would pass 2♡ like a shot. When opener bids the suit that partner transfers to, he may hate it. When he likes it, he should say so. Always remember to support with support.

	West	North	East	South
♠ K53	—	—	—	4♡
♡ 6	P	P	???	
◇ A74				
♣ AKJ1063				

Double. Not easy, but I prefer the flexible double to the over-optimistic 5♣ and the ultra-conservative pass.

Partner can bid or pass, depending on his hand. On most hands, the five level belongs to the opponents.

	West	North	East	South
♠ Q64	—	4♡	P	P
♡ —	Dbl	P	???	
◇ Q8543				
♣ J7432				

Bid 4NT, promising both minors. Do not defend 4♡ doubled when the opponents have so many hearts.

If the opponents are happy in 4♡ with ten or more trumps, your side must be unhappy. We expect to do just fine in partner's better minor. Voids are wonderful for offense.

No topic is more important for improving your game than The Law of Total Tricks. Does that make this a formidable subject? Fortunately not. All you need is an open mind and a little arithmetic.

Don't Think Twice—Bid 4♠ Over 4♡

Scene: Finals, National Swiss Teams (three-day event).
Seattle, Washington, November 28, 1993.

Auction: Pass 1♣ 4♡ ???

Your hand: ♠ 10876432 ♡ 2 ◇ 86 ♣ A54

Vulnerability: Vulnerable against not.

What did I do? For years, I have been preaching the necessity of bidding 4♠ over 4♡ whenever rational. Although many players might question the rationality of bidding at these colors with a four-point hand and a suit headed by the ten, all I can say is: "Faint heart never won fair maiden." I duly bid 4♠, and here was the layout:

North (Marty)
♠ 10876432
♡ 2
◇ 86
♣ A54

West		*East*
♠ 9	5♡ Dbl	♠ AJ
♡ AKQJ85	♣A LEAD	♡ 10764
◇ KQJ3		◇ 1075
♣ Q6		♣ 9873

South
♠ KQ5
♡ 93
◇ A942
♣ KJ102

West	North	East	South
—	—	P	1♣
4♡	4♠	5♡	P
P	Dbl	all pass	

Notice the effect of the 4♠ bid. East-West were about to play a cozy 4♡, easily scoring ten tricks for + 420. Over 4♠ East had an obvious 5♡ bid, which was doubled for down one. Even if a little bird had whispered into East's ear and had told him to defend 4♠, the best he would have been able to do was beat it one after declarer's normal club misguess.

As this deal illustrates, four-level actions can be crucial. I would like to demonstrate that there is a lot more to this subject than the final decision after 4♥. Frequently the early bird catches the matchpoints.

One way to approach this dilemma was discussed in Larry Cohen's best-selling book, *To Bid or Not to Bid: The LAW of Total Tricks*. Larry taught players to appreciate their trump length and to accept that The LAW is more important than HCP when it comes to competitive bidding.

Let us take a look at another example. You are South and open 1♠. Before you know it, the auction has accelerated to the three level. What call do you make?

		West	North	East	South
♠	KQ10743	—	—	—	1♠
♥	8	2♥	2♠	3♥	???
♦	KQ106				
♣	93				

Many players would compete with 3♠, and I too would be pleased to declare that contract. But is that really likely? The opponents are probably about to bid 4♥. Do you have any interest in defending that contract? Not me, I would rather bid 4♠. If it makes, great. If it does not, it will cost me less than the score for the opponents making 4♥.

Another reason for the immediate 4♠ bid is that if you wait until later, the enemy will be in a better position to judge to double you, or on occasion bid 5♥. You put a great deal of pressure on West if you bid 4♠ immediately. He will have to judge unilaterally whether to bid, pass or double.

Some alert LAW-abiding readers may question bidding at the four level with only nine trumps. However, because both 4♥ and 4♠ represent game contracts, the potential gain for both sides is great. If partner has the following hand...

♠ A92   ♥ 764   ◇ A853   ♣ 742

...it is likely that both games are cold.

Finally, try this hand, also from the Seattle Nationals. With neither side vulnerable you are North, gazing at this lovely collection:

♠ 10653
♡ 85
◇ 108743
♣ J3

Partner opens 1♠ and your RHO doubles. Do you appreciate your nine-card fit? The LAW is telling you to make a preemptive jump to 3♠. Would you?

North
♠ 10653
♡ 85
◇ 108743
♣ J3

West
♠ 9
♡ KQJ7
◇ AQ5
♣ A10964

5♡
♠A LEAD

East
♠ KJ
♡ A10942
◇ KJ2
♣ 872

South
♠ AQ8742
♡ 63
◇ 96
♣ KQ5

West	North	East	South
—	—	—	1♠
Dbl	3♠	4♡	4♠
5♡	all pass		

The 5♡ contract went down one[1]. The key was North's preemptive 3♠ bid. I do not believe that any of the actions taken by East-West can be criticized. They were just unlucky to be missing a crucial club honor. Of course, they were also unlucky to be playing against this particular North-South pair, who understood the advantages of bidding 4♠ over 4♡.

---

[1]Even if East-West had known to double 4♠, it should go down only two. Declarer can force an entry to dummy for the winning spade finesse (the correct play with ten cards missing the king is to finesse). If the ♣J does not get him there, he can still ruff a winning club.

CHAPTER 12
Counting Your Way to the Top

This Dummy Knows it All

As North, you are dealt this lousy hand, with both sides vulnerable:

♠ Q
♡ J642
◇ 1098654
♣ J3

Whatever thoughts of competing you may have entertained are dashed when your RHO opens 1◇. You pass and the auction continues:

West	You	East	South
1◇	P	1NT	2♣
all pass			

You are wondering what happened to the spade suit when the auction comes to a screeching halt.

As the 1◇ bidder ponders his opening lead, you have nothing better to do than consider the auction. Can you deduce what is going on? I suggest you take a moment to reflect before reading further.

Begin with the spade suit. Opener clearly denied five of them, and responder could have bid a four-card suit. When East chose 1NT instead, he denied a four-card major, so he has at most three. If East-West do not have eight spades, South must have at least five of them. He certainly would have overcalled with a six-card suit, so he has exactly five. Therefore, you are confident that the spades are distributed as follows:

North (You)
♠ one card

West
♠ four cards

East
♠ three cards

South
♠ five cards

With five spades and five clubs, South would have overcalled 2♠, his higher-ranking suit. Therefore, I am going to assign him six or seven clubs. That leaves him with only one or two cards in the red suits.

What about hearts, the other major? We can apply the same logic we used for spades to count the hearts. The East-West auction denied an eight-card fit, so South must have two hearts.

Since we have established that South has at least 11 black cards, we know his entire distribution. He was dealt:

♠ five cards   ♡ two cards   ◇ none   ♣ six cards

Now for the opponents. Opener (West) has four cards in each major, and East must have three. What about diamonds? We cannot be 100% positive about that suit, but it is reasonable to assume that East would have supported opener's 1◇ opening sooner or later if he had four of them. Therefore, East should have at most three diamonds.

Can East have only two diamonds, and therefore five clubs? Probably not. East might have doubled 2♣ with that many of them. If he had five, West would have been void, and he would not have passed with 4-4-5-0 distribution. He would have bid 2◇ over 2♣. Eureka, we know it all.

By the way, once dummy was tabled, all of the above information was available to each of the other players.

For those who like no loose ends, here is the entire deal:

North (You)
♠ Q
♡ J642
◇ 1098654
♣ J3

West
♠ K984
♡ K873
◇ AKJ7
♣ 10

```
┌─────────┐
│   2♣    │
│ ◇A LEAD │
└─────────┘
```

East
♠ J102
♡ Q109
◇ Q32
♣ A852

South
♠ A7653
♡ A5
◇ —
♣ KQ9764

(Repeated for convenience)

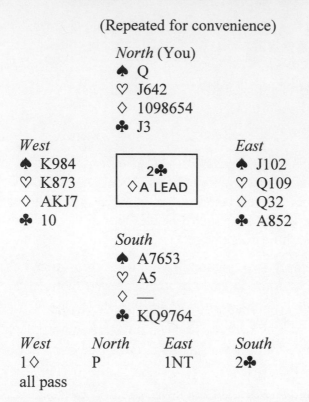

North (You)
♠ Q
♡ J642
◇ 1098654
♣ J3

West
♠ K984
♡ K873
◇ AKJ7
♣ 10

2♣
◇A LEAD

East
♠ J102
♡ Q109
◇ Q32
♣ A852

South
♠ A7653
♡ A5
◇ —
♣ KQ9764

West	*North*	*East*	*South*
1◇	P	1NT	2♣
all pass			

The story had a happy ending for North-South. Declarer trumped West's normal diamond lead and ruffed two spades on the board as quickly as he could. He was now able to score an overtrick, winning his two aces, two ruffs in dummy and five trumps in his own hand. If West had known to lead a trump, perfect defense would have resulted in a plus score for East-West.

Junior Bids Up the Line

There are three bridge players sitting around waiting for their fourth to show up. They are about to give up when one of their children walks into the room. They grab him, give him about two minutes of bridge instruction and down he sits. With a pile of cookies in front of him, he is happy to oblige.

Our little hero is thrilled to correctly deal 13 cards to each player and even happier when he learns that he gets to bid first. "**Four** clubs," he says. Everyone at the table looks aghast and his LHO (dear mother) doubles, and it goes pass, pass back to him. No problem. The kid bids **four** diamonds and lo and behold, more funny looks and another double. Pass, pass back to junior. He is unabashed. "**Four** hearts" he chirps. Once again it goes double, pass, pass. Junior is thrilled. "And **one** spade."

Puzzle Solving

In this article, I would like to discuss counting—an ability that separates bridge players from **bridge players**.

In class one day, two of my better students had the following auction (the opponents passed throughout):

North	South	
North	*South*	Clubs were led and declarer (South) trumped the second
—	1◇	round. At this point, it is possible to figure out declarer's
1♡	1♠	exact distribution. When defending, this information is
2◇	2♡	crucial. If you would like to challenge yourself, take a
3◇	P	moment to count declarer's distribution.

Treat this as a puzzle. The first piece is that declarer has only one club. The next piece involves the spade suit—we consider it now because we have lots of information about it already. South did not open 1♠, so he does not have five. Because he bid the suit over partner's 1♡ response, he must have exactly four.

That leaves South with eight cards in the red suits. We should tackle hearts next. Although some might think that declarer has four hearts, that is not correct. If he did have four, he would have raised hearts immediately. Once he found a four-four major-suit fit, he would not go looking for another fit. Therefore, he has exactly three hearts.

Are you surprised? Why would South support hearts with only three of them? Because North's 2◇ bid did not deny five hearts. To bid 2♡ at his second turn, North would have needed a six-card heart suit. Therefore, South employs good technique by bidding 2♡. Reminder: it is opener's duty to show his three-card support for responder's major at some point. If responder has only four cards, he is allowed to retreat.

Now, and only now can we count diamonds confidently. With everything else in place, this is easy. We know that South has one club, four spades and three hearts, leaving him with five diamonds. The exact distribution of declarer's hand is 4-3-5-1!

Because we are looking at dummy, we know the distribution of three of the four players' hands at the table. Figuring out the fourth is just a matter of concentration.

Try another one—a bit more challenging this time. At a recent duplicate, I was trying to stay awake while gazing at the following Yarborough:

	West	North	Me	South
♠ 742	—	—	—	1♠
♡ 98632	P	2♡	P	3NT
◇ 643	all pass			
♣ 96				

My partner led the ♣3. This is what I saw:

North (dummy)
♠ 65
♡ AKQ74
◇ J5
♣ J842

3NT
♣3 LEAD

East (Marty)
♠ 742
♡ 98632
◇ 643
♣ 96

Although I did not approve of declarer's bidding, I was able to figure out his entire distribution at trick one. You can too. Let's do it!

The obvious suit to begin with is clubs, the suit led. Partner must have at least four of them to justify the lead against 3NT. It is not possible for him to have a five-card suit because the only club below his three is sitting in dummy. So, partner has four clubs, dummy has four, and I have two. Therefore, declarer must have exactly three.

Now take a look at the spade suit. It is reasonable to assume that South has just five of them because he never rebid the suit. With three clubs and five spades, declarer must have five cards in diamonds and hearts. Because he rebid 3NT, his most likely distribution of these two suits is three-two. Once North promised five hearts with his 2♡ bid, South should have only two. We now know declarer's precise distribution: 5-2-3-3. Well done!

Time out!! There is a fly in the ointment. If you can spot it, you are already a **player**. Care to take a moment to reexamine the clues?

If South really has the distribution we assigned him, West would have to have five diamonds! (There are two in dummy, three in declarer's hand and three in my hand). Would he lead from a four-card club suit when he had five diamonds? No, he would not. We must now adjust our view of declarer's hand. He must have four diamonds and only one heart: 5-1-4-3. Good detective work!

Declarer's actual hand was:

♠ AQJ83   ♡ 10   ◇ AK102   ♣ K105

As I mentioned earlier, I definitely would not have rebid 3NT after partner's 2♡ response. My auction would have begun:

West	North	East	South
—	—	—	1♠
P	2♡	P	3◇

That is hardly the point. This is: "Counting to a bridge player is similar to an actor learning his lines—it does not guarantee success, but he cannot succeed without it." That bit of wisdom comes from George S. Kaufman, evidently a man of many talents.

CHAPTER 13
Overcoming the Opposition

Dear Marty

Dear Marty: Bridge players can be so rude. After going down in 4♠ yesterday, I was told by one of my opponents that I could have used a Bath Coup! What a thing to say? I was mortified. I assured her that I shower every morning, but she laughed and said that she was only talking about the play of the hand. What a relief! Please help me. Here is the hand:

North
- ♠ 1096
- ♡ 865
- ◇ QJ62
- ♣ AK5

```
    4♠
  ♡K LEAD
```

South
- ♠ KQJ872
- ♡ AJ4
- ◇ K5
- ♣ 109

    The king of hearts was led. I won the ace and led the king of diamonds, hoping to get rid of my heart losers on dummy's diamonds. It didn't work, though. East won the ace and returned a heart and I lost two hearts and the ace of trumps. What did I do wrong?

Confused in Charleston

Dear Confused but Clean: Good news. I can answer both question because they are one and the same. Your opponent was saying that you should have ducked the ♡K at the first trick. Now, if your LHO continues hearts into your AJ, you will not lose a second heart trick. That is all there is to the Bath Coup. It is 100% a bridge term, not a reflection on your personal hygiene.

While that holdup play would not guarantee your contract, it does represent your best chance.

Dear Marty: I am an experienced duplicate player, but I came across something the other day that was a new one on me. While I was dummy, I noticed that one of my opponents had printed "Snapdragon" in big letters on her convention card under "Doubles." I couldn't wait to ask her what it was, but she said that she had no idea!

Her friend had told her about it a while ago, and she loved the sound of the word, so she always wrote it on her card. I am very curious. Is there such a convention?

C. G. in Destin, Florida

Dear Curious: Yes, there is a Snapdragon double. After three players have bid their suits, a double by the fourth player promises five cards in the unbid suit as well as tolerance for partner's suit. Tolerance is usually two cards, often with an honor. The five-card suit would not be strong, otherwise you would just bid your suit. Here is an example auction. Suppose you are South:

West	North	East	South
1♣	1♦	1♠	Dbl

Make a Snapdragon double, promising hearts with diamond tolerance with:

♠ 85   ♡ Q7643   ◊ A8   ♣ A643

♠ AJ4   ♡ K10852   ◊ 982   ♣ 86

However, holding...

♠ 64   ♡ KQJ87   ◊ K5   ♣ 9865

...just bid 2♡.

Some players refer to this kind of double as negative, but that is incorrect. Negative doubles can only be made in response to partner's opening bid. Should everyone use Snapdragon? No, because the potential for accidents is great. However, since doubling the opponents' forcing bid for penalty makes no sense, Snapdragon is a convention that I recommend for experienced players.

I have also heard experts refer to these doubles as "third-suit doubles" and "fourth-suit doubles." While either is certainly reasonable, I agree with your opponent's choice. "Snapdragon" sounds a whole lot better.

Same Hand, Different Auction

One of the most important concepts you can learn about the game of bridge is that "little things mean a lot." Allow me to explain. You are dealt:

```
♠ 1092
♡ KQ10984
◇ J43
♣ 4
```

You are all set to open 2♡, but alas, you are not the dealer.

Here are 20 auctions where you must decide what to do with this hand. Neither side is vulnerable. You get five points for each correct answer.

Several conventions will rear their heads on these auctions, and obviously not everyone has identical agreements. I will try to limit my use of conventions to those that are most popular.

For each auction, you are the player with the "???".

West	North	East	South
1♡	P	???	

Bid 4♡. As easy as it gets.

West	North	East	South
1♣	???		

Bid 2♡, a weak jump overcall. This is first-cousin to opening a weak two-bid.

West	North	East	South
1♠	P	???	

Raise to 2♠. Because your hand is not nearly strong enough to bid 2♡, you will show your support for partner's major.

West	North	East	South
1♢	1♠	???	

Bid 3♡, a weak jump shift in competition. This treatment is recommended for players of all levels. It is rare enough to be dealt the 17 points you need to jump shift after partner opens, but it is even rarer once the opponents get into the auction.

West	North	East	South
1♣	Dbl	???	

Bid 2♡, another example of the weak jump shift in competition.

West	North	East	South
1NT	P	???	

Bid 2♢, a Jacoby transfer.

West	North	East	South
1♡	2♡	P	???

Bid 2♠, taking a preference for partner's five-card spade suit, which he promised by bidding Michaels.

West	North	East	South
1♣	P	1♡	3♢
P	P	???	

Pass. Your hand is not good enough to take another bid at the three level. Your possible misfit clinches the pass. Just go quietly.

West	North	East	South
1NT	Dbl*	???	

Alerted as artificial.

Bid 2♢, a Jacoby transfer. It is recommended that you play "system on" after an artificial double. Make sure you and partner agree about your methods here.

♠ 1092
♡ KQ10984
◇ J43
♣ 4

West	North	East	South
3◇	3♠	???	

Raise to 4◇. Support with support. Do not allow your LHO to bid either 3NT or 4♣. If 4◇ is doubled (unlikely since your partnership has ten of them), you expect to survive based on The LAW.

West	North	East	South
1♣	1NT	???	

Bid 2♡, a weak bid. After the opponent's 1NT overcall, your only strength-showing action is double.

West	North	East	South
1♣	P	P	???

Balance with 1♡. In this position, a jump overcall would promise an opening bid.

West	North	East	South
1◇	2♠	P	P
Dbl	P	???	

Jump to 4♡. You would have bid 3♡ with five small hearts and one HCP.

West	North	East	South
3♠	P	???	

Raise to 4♠. Your partnership has ten spades and you are happy to bid to the four level.

West	North	East	South
3♣	P	???	

Pass. Playing standard bridge, a new suit is forcing after partner preempts. I prefer the new suit to be nonforcing. Every partnership must arrange a meeting of the minds on this non-trivial issue.

West	North	East	South
1NT	P	P	???

Do not pass at any vulnerability. If playing DONT, you would double to show a one-suited hand. Using natural methods, bid 2♥.

West	North	East	South
1♠	1NT	2♦	???

Bid 2♥. This is natural and competitive. If partner raises, you will go on to game.

West	North	East	South
1♠	2NT	P	???

Bid 3♦ after the unusual notrump. Partner never promised any hearts, just minors. Take a preference.

West	North	East	South
1♦	Dbl	Rdbl	???

Jump to 3♥. After the redouble, all bids by fourth hand say nothing about strength. I would happily bid 3♥ even if the ♥K were the deuce. It's The LAW.

West	North	East	South
3♣	Dbl	4♣	???

Bid 4♥. Partner forced you to respond 3♥ with a complete Yarborough and four hearts. With this hand, you have no qualms about bidding one level higher.

Twenty auctions with our one hand. If you got 13 right, you did fine. To those who got 18 (or more) right, my compliments.

Seeking a Happy Medium

What do you think of the following? **Most players bid too much or too little on most hands.**

That statement might not be politically correct, but it is based on more than three decades of teaching and playing experience.

Too often, players overbid with good hands and underbid with bad ones. They fall in love with nice hands and turn off with poor ones.

Here is your opportunity to do better. With both sides vulnerable, you are North and pick up:

	West	North	East	South
♠ 7542	—	—	P	1♡
♡ K107	1♠	P	2♠	3◇
◇ 85	P	???		
♣ 8653				

How do you feel about your modest collection? What is your bid?

I **hope** you bid 4♡. From where I sit, the North hand has no less than four positive features: the two heart honors, the third heart and the doubleton diamond. Not bad for a hand with three HCP. The entire deal:

North
♠ 7542
♡ K107
◇ 85
♣ 8653

West
♠ AKJ86
♡ 63
◇ Q3
♣ Q1074

4♡
♠A LEAD

East
♠ 1093
♡ 942
◇ 10764
♣ AKJ

South
♠ Q
♡ AQJ85
◇ AKJ92
♣ 92

Notice that 4♡ is easy to make. If you believe that South should go on even if North only takes a preference to 3♡, I totally disagree. North would have bid 3♡ with either of the following hands:

♠ 10874   ♡ 743   ◇ 743   ♣ QJ8

♠ K743   ♡ 92   ◇ 7   ♣ J87653

You can see that 4♡ would be an awful contract opposite these dummies. Remember, partner's preference was no stronger than a pass.

Now try this one. Once again you are North, this time only your side is vulnerable. The auction has begun:

West	North	East	South
—	—	—	1◇
P	1♠	P	2♣
P	2♠	P	3♣
P	???		

♠ J109843
♡ 5
◇ A8
♣ J1052

What do we know about partner's hand? He is at least five-five in the minors and he hates your spades. The opponent's silence is meaningful; with at least nine hearts between them, they would have bid something if they had the balance of power.

What (if anything) would you do? Make your decision before reading on.

Here is the entire deal:

North (You)
♠ J109843
♡ 5
♢ A8
♣ J1052

West		*East*
♠ A72	5♣	♠ KQ65
♡ KQ63	♡K LEAD	♡ A10874
♢ 10532		♢ J9
♣ 98		♣ 64

South
♠ —
♡ J92
♢ KQ764
♣ AKQ73

West	North	East	South
—	—	—	1♢
P	1♠	P	2♣
P	2♠	P	3♣
P	???		

I hope that you left nothing to chance. The correct bid was 5♣. Once South bid 3♣, North should have realized that his modest collection had turned to solid gold.

Are you ready for a good hand?

	You	*Partner*
♠ K	2♣	2♢
♡ KJ654	2♡	3♣*
♢ AKQ4	3♢	3♡
♣ AKJ	???	

* Second negative.

You have 24 HCP, a bit more than your normal allotment. Your first three bids are automatic. Now what? Partner showed a very bad hand (0-3 HCP) with his 3♣ rebid. After bidding 3♡, what is he likely to have?

♠ 9854   ♡ Q98   ◇ J102   ♣ 864

I think not. After his 3♣ denial, partner should appreciate his honor-third of hearts and his two diamond honors and jump to 4♡.

How about this one?

♠ QJ87   ♡ 73   ◇ 105   ♣ 109743

Again, no. With this he would bid 3NT over 3◇.

♠ Q643   ♡ 83   ◇ 973   ♣ 7643

This one is quite possible. Partner had to bid **something** after our forcing 3◇ bid. In fact, his ♠Q could have been the deuce.

Do not be blinded by your 24 HCP. You began the day with the sun shining brightly, but now all you can see are grey clouds and rain. Your correct action is to pass 3♡ and hope you make it.

Finally, take a look at this collection:

♠ —
♡ AKQ
◇ KJ54
♣ KJ7643

Nice hand, lots of potential. You are West and open 1♣ as dealer. The auction proceeds.

West	North	East	South
1♣	1◇	1♠	P
???			

Not what you were hoping for? North is sitting behind you with diamond length and strength, which greatly reduces the potential of your second suit. Partner's spade bid does nothing for you either.

Unless partner has a club fit, where are your tricks coming from? It is time to take the low road. Your correct bid is a modest 2♣. In fact, if partner holds something like...

♠ AQJ93   ♡ 8652   ◇ 732   ♣ 9

...I have my doubts as to whether you can take eight tricks. If you are aware of a good line of play in 2♣ after a passive heart lead, perhaps you should be writing this book instead of reading it.

CHAPTER 14
The Bad Guys Go First

What's Your Call?

For each hand, RHO opens 1♠. You are vulnerable and the opponents are not. What is your call?

♠ QJ63
♡ K
♢ K9532
♣ KQ7

Pass. You may be impressed with your 14 HCP, but I do not like the looks of this hand. Your spades will be far more useful on defense than offense, and the same is true of your ♡K. Two-level overcalls and king-empty-fifth do not belong in the same sentence.

♠ —
♡ A10982
♢ KJ1087
♣ 763

Overcall 2♠, a Michaels cuebid. When you have a void, strive to take action. You love your five-five distribution and nice intermediate cards.

♠ 5
♡ 5
♢ KQJ7643
♣ J873

Bid 3♢. Do not stop preempting at unfavorable vulnerability. Ultimately, "bridge is bridge." You are unhappy when your opponents preempt and you have to guess what to do. Therefore, strive to return the favor when opportunity knocks.

♠ 75
♡ A109832
♢ KQ87
♣ 3

2♡ is a very normal overcall. It should not bother you that you have only nine HCP. You have great shape and a nice six-card suit.

Double. I love to bid five-card majors, but over-calling at the two level with such a weak suit is just begging for trouble.

Double again. This hand is far too good for a mere 2♣ overcall. You hope that partner will respond 1NT so that you can raise to game. Otherwise, you will bid your clubs next. When you double then bid your own suit, you show a big hand.

Double. This hand will make a lovely dummy for partner no matter what suit he bids.

Bid 3NT. On a spade lead, nine tricks are very likely. If you wait for a surer proposition, you are sure to miss the boat.

Double. If partner responds 2◇, you will have to pass and hold your breath. However, that is no reason to bury your head in the sand. A 2♣ overcall with such anemic clubs is more dangerous than double and has no upside. Your best chance for a future is in a major.

Pass. A jump to 2NT at this vulnerability is not unusual—it is suicidal. Your suits lack texture and your seven HCP in the majors are not pulling their weight. If you pass and LHO's 2♠ bid is passed around to you, then you will balance with 2NT.

Remember, RHO opened 1♠.

♠ KQJ6
♡ 7
♢ J8643
♣ AK6

Pass. You might think that I left my bidding shoes at home on this one. Not so. In fact, I am always eager to take action. However, with length and strength in the opponent's suit, a discreet pass is clear.

♠ QJ
♡ KJ5
♢ KJ64
♣ KJ42

Pass this one also. You are not proud of your three points in spades and it is not mandatory to overcall just because you have 15 HCP. This hand is full of... jacks and has almost no trick-taking potential. Keep quiet.

Twelve hands, twelve opportunities to overcall. We passed four of them with 14, 12, 14 and 15 HCP. We took action on four of them with eight, seven, nine and nine HCP.

Perhaps that means that HCP are not the key to overcall decisions. Perhaps there is even a phrase to summarize this. Two words with the initials "P.S." come to mind.

DONT Miss This Tip

As players become more experienced, they learn that conventions are necessary. Negative doubles, limit raises, weak two-bids and Jacoby transfers are all living proof of that.

For most players, bidding after an opponent opens 1NT is a very misunderstood topic. Players are busy counting points, and trying to guess which suit to bid with a hand like this one:

	West	*You*	*East*	*South*
♠ 98	1NT	???		
♡ KJ764				
◇ A				
♣ KJ943				

Those days can be over. As long as you have an open mind, I believe that DONT will appeal to you. Ever since I invented this convention in 1981, it has proven to be a consistent winner. DONT has been well received by both intermediate and advanced players.

Here are the principles that led to the invention of Bergen Over Notrump, now better known as DONT (**D**isturbing the **O**pponent's **N**o**T**rump):

✓ Two-suited hands occur more frequently than their one-suited counterparts. When your hand is two-suited and you can say so, partner will help get the partnership to the right spot.

✓ Defending against 1NT is usually not in your best interest. The opening lead is often an annoying guess. Subsequent leads and discards can result in a loss of sleep as well.

✓ Because this convention allows you to show every distributional hand type, you can **D**isturb the **O**pponent's **N**o**T**rump frequently.

✓ It is not necessary to have a method to penalize an opponent's 1NT opening. In the first place, you seldom are dealt that good a hand. Second, your penalty double may allow the opponents to find a better contract.

When using DONT, remember the following tips:

✓ **_Points schmoints._** Distribution and vulnerability are the keys, as in all overcall situations.

✓ Most of the time, you are not trying to get to game; you only wish to enter the auction when you have good shape.

✓ DONT applies in both direct and balancing seats, as long as 1NT was the last bid. In the balancing seat, its strength requirements are greatly relaxed.

✓ With strong balanced hands, **pass**, **Pass**, **PASS** (trust me).

DONT

With a hand that merits action, proceed as follows. With a two-suited hand (five-four or longer), bid the cheaper of your suits:

   2♣ shows clubs and a second suit.
   2♢ shows diamonds and a higher suit (obviously a major).
   2♡ shows hearts and a higher suit (spades).

With a one-suited hand, usually six cards long:

   2♠ shows spades (surprise!).
   Double shows clubs or diamonds or hearts.

Here are some examples. All alertable actions will be designated with an asterisk. At any vulnerability after RHO opens 1NT,

bid 2♣* with:

♠ KJ954   ♡ 8   ♢ 63   ♣ K10976

♠ 75   ♡ AQ862   ♢ 63   ♣ KQ109

bid 2♢* with:

♠ AJ97   ♡ 6   ♢ KQ976   ♣ K64

♠ 6   ♡ K7543   ♢ AJ865   ♣ Q3

bid 2♡* with:

> ♠ KQJ9 ♡ A10954 ◇ 6 ♣ 764
>
> ♠ A9865 ♡ KJ975 ◇ J6 ♣ 8

bid 2♠ with:

> ♠ KQ10875 ♡ 4 ◇ 9865 ♣ A2
>
> ♠ AQ9754 ♡ 987 ◇ AJ8 ♣ 7

double* with:

> ♠ J76 ♡ KQJ643 ◇ K76 ♣ 8
>
> ♠ 6 ♡ K7 ◇ AQJ754 ♣ J654
>
> ♠ 9762 ♡ A5 ◇ 7 ♣ AJ10973

Responses to DONT

If partner doubles:
> Bid 2♣ so that he can identify his long suit easily.

If partner overcalls 2♣ or 2◇ showing the lower-ranking suit of a two-suited hand:
> Pass with three or more cards in partner's bid suit.
> Bid your own strong suit with six or more cards.
> Otherwise, make the cheapest bid (alertable), which asks partner to bid his second suit.

If partner overcalls 2♡ showing both majors:
> Choose your better major at the appropriate level.

Now, try your hand at responding to DONT. The auction has proceeded as follows (you are South):

West	North	East	South
1NT	2♣*	P	???

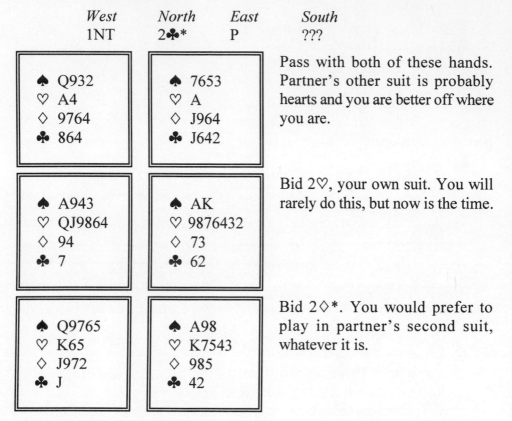

♠ Q932
♡ A4
♦ 9764
♣ 864

♠ 7653
♡ A
♦ J964
♣ J642

Pass with both of these hands. Partner's other suit is probably hearts and you are better off where you are.

♠ A943
♡ QJ9864
♦ 94
♣ 7

♠ AK
♡ 9876432
♦ 73
♣ 62

Bid 2♡, your own suit. You will rarely do this, but now is the time.

♠ Q9765
♡ K65
♦ J972
♣ J

♠ A98
♡ K7543
♦ 985
♣ 42

Bid 2♦*. You would prefer to play in partner's second suit, whatever it is.

You are North, the DONT bidder.

West	North	East	South
1NT	2♣*	P	2♦*
P	???		

♠ K4
♡ 82
♦ A10643
♣ KQ109

Pass. Partner hit your second suit with his inquiry.

♠ J43	♠ K10432
♡ A1082	♡ A
◇ 6	◇ 86
♣ AK975	♣ K9765

With both these hands, simply bid your second suit, as requested. Bid 2♡ with the first hand; 2♠ with the second.

Here are some examples of DONT in action. You might enjoy covering up the auction in the middle and bidding these hands with your favorite partner. South opens 1NT.

West (Overcaller)			*East* (Responder)
♠ Q63	2♣*	2◇*	♠ K742
♡ KJ73	2♡	P	♡ Q84
◇ A			◇ 97532
♣ A7643			♣ 8

After the 2♣ overcall, East wishes to escape from clubs. His 2◇ response asks partner to bid his other suit. Will the opponents be smart enough to lead trumps?

♠ A84	Dbl*	2♣*	♠ KJ73
♡ 5	2◇	P	♡ J842
◇ AKJ843			◇ 6
♣ Q83			♣ J954

The double shows one long suit. East inquires via 2♣ and allows partner to bid his lovely diamonds.

♠ 6	3♡	4♡	♠ A9753
♡ KQJ8754	P		♡ 632
◇ 864			◇ AK7
♣ 74			♣ A6

With a beautiful seven-card suit and no defense, West is delighted to preempt the auction to the three level ASAP. East is happy to raise with nice support and four quick tricks.

South opens 1NT.

West (Overcaller)			*East* (Responder)
♠ A8643	2♡*	3♠	♠ KJ72
♡ AQ853	4♠	P	♡ J10
◇ 864			◇ A93
♣ —			♣ 8743

After West promises the majors, East's hand sure looks good. With a conservative partner, he would simply jump to game himself. West has no problem accepting East's invitation and proceeding to the laydown game.

♠ K743	P	2♣*	♠ 85
♡ 953	2◇*	2♡	♡ J8742
◇ AKQ8	P		◇ 7
♣ KJ			♣ Q9764

Would *you* be able to pass 1NT with West's 16-point hand? Experience has shown that it is the best action. East is eager to balance with his shapely hand, knowing that partner must have the missing points. West is disappointed that partner's second suit is hearts, and sensibly passes in the best contract.

♠ 6	2◇*	2♠	♠ QJ10853
♡ AQ107	P		♡ K5
◇ KJ873			◇ 92
♣ 873			♣ K92

With two nice suits, West is pleased to disturb the opponent's notrump. East expects that partner's second suit is hearts and overrules with his 2♠ bid. West trusts his partner and calls it a day.

♠ AK987	2◇*	2♡*	♠ Q532
♡ 8	3♠	4♠	♡ 9653
◇ AQ983	P		◇ 7
♣ J3			♣ A982

With his very strong hand, West jumps to 3♠. That is all East needs to raise to game.

West (Overcaller)			*East* (Responder)
♠ AJ832	2◇*	2♡*	♠ 9
♡ 6	2♠	3♣	♡ A9542
◇ KQ1083	P		◇ 6
♣ Q7			♣ KJ10983

Uh oh, could be a misfit. East knew that West's second suit was spades, but hoped that his clubs represented the best of a bad lot.

♠ K843	Dbl*	2♣*	♠ Q92
♡ A4	2◇	P	♡ K942
◇ KQJ943			◇ 7
♣ 8			♣ K9732

With six-four distribution, I suggest emphasizing the long suit when playing DONT. The 2◇ contract looks a lot more playable than 2♠.

Armed with your new weapon, you are now poised to disturb and compete. Trust me, you don't want to play bridge without DONT.

Some Hands Get Better With Age

With everyone vulnerable, you are sitting South and pick up:

	West	North	East	South (You)
♠ 7	—	—	1NT	P
♡ J742	2♡*	Dbl	2♠	???
◇ AQ32				
♣ AQJ5				

2♡ is alerted as Jacoby.

You recognize partner's double as lead directing, promising length and strength in hearts. As expected, opener now bids 2♠.

It is time for an important aside. Did you know that experienced players assign a meaning to opener's free 2♠ bid (as opposed to a forced 2♠ bid without the double)? Because of the double, opener now has the option of passing with only two spades. Therefore, the 2♠ bid on this auction promises at least three spades. So much for East-West, back to your hand.

Do you believe your pretty little collection merits any action?

Okay, now that you have made your decision, read on. Partner promised at least five good hearts. Your ace-queens look very nice behind the notrump opener. Your spade singleton insures no more than one loser in that suit. It is good bridge to support partner when he shows a suit you love.

If you bid 3♡, you are on the right track. However, if you want to impress me, jump to 4♡.

Take a look at the entire deal:

North
♠ A84
♡ K10983
♢ 94
♣ 742

West
♠ K10963
♡ 5
♢ 10865
♣ 1086

```
┌─────────────┐
│     4♡      │
│  ♡5 LEAD    │
└─────────────┘
```

East
♠ QJ52
♡ AQ6
♢ KJ7
♣ K93

South
♠ 7
♡ J742
♢ AQ32
♣ AQJ5

West	North	East	South
—	—	1NT	P
2♡*	Dbl	2♠	4♡
all pass			

* *2♡ is alerted as Jacoby.*

Since East opened 1NT and South must have a distributional hand to bid this way, West should lead a trump. As it turns out, because both minor-suit kings are in the pocket, 4♡ is cold. In fact, South should make five. If East-West attempt to sacrifice in 4♠, they will get doubled and good defense will result in down three (800) when North eventually ruffs a diamond.

Not many bridge players would know to double 2♡ with North's hand. I am confident that it is the winning action because the importance of helping partner find the best lead cannot be overemphasized.

If you have never bid after a lead-directing double, I hope that this hand got you thinking. Many players probably cannot even remember the last time they made a lead-directing double. So much for their misguided past. Out with the old, dull passes, in with the new bids and doubles. To quote the Academy Award-winning song from *Aladdin*: it's "A Whole New World."

Balancing Knowhow

Although I am not sure why this is so, I have learned over the years that many bridge players are not aware of the significant differences between actions in direct and balancing seats.

You are South with both sides vulnerable. Your auction is as follows:

West	North	East	South
1◇	P	P	???

♠ 853
♡ Q10942
◇ 4
♣ KJ42

Bid 1♡. Where are the points? With East having fewer than six, partner is marked with a good hand. Why didn't he bid? He had the wrong distribution. His hand probably looks something like:

♠ A74   ♡ K3   ◇ AQ93   ♣ 10983

It was crucial to prevent the opponents from playing a comfortable 1◇. Not only was it perfectly safe to balance with 1♡, it was your responsibility. An essential principle of competitive bidding is that the hand that is short in the opponent's suit is the one that should strain to take action.

♠ K53
♡ K2
◇ AJ6
♣ 97432

1NT is your bid. Because we try so hard to act in balancing seat, less strength is required than when you overcall 1NT directly. Therefore, instead of 15-18 HCP, **1NT in balancing seat shows 10-14 HCP**.

You are counting on partner to furnish enough help to make the contract playable. By not selling out, you have given yourself a good chance to push the opponents up to a contract they cannot make.

♠ A8
♡ KQ8432
◇ 83
♣ K92

Bid 2♡! I know, I know, you play weak jump overcalls. So do I, but they do not apply when balancing.

In balancing seat, jump overcalls are defined as intermediate. They promise a good six-card suit and a hand strong enough to open.

If I had a nickel for every player who does not know this, I would have more money than my wife could spend.

♠ A743
♡ A93
♢ 82
♣ Q1076

Double. You would not have enough to double in direct seat, but that is not the situation. You must protect partner in this position, and are prepared for any action that he might take.

♠ KQJ9
♡ 83
♢ A5
♣ 87432

Bid 1♠. This is the same bid I would make in direct seat. Your spades look a lot better than that miserable club suit. You must not allow the auction to die without a fight.

♠ AQ
♡ AJ84
♢ A62
♣ J1074

Double. Remember that a balancing 1NT shows only 10-14 HCP—this hand is stronger than that. Therefore, you must double. If partner responds 1♠, you will rebid 1NT with your nice hand.

♠ 7
♡ AJ93
♢ KQ105
♣ K732

Pass. You do not mind if the opponents play in diamonds when you have a strong holding in their trump suit. If you keep the auction alive by balancing, someone is going to introduce spades. Regardless of who that is, you will not be happy.

♠ K104
♡ A73
♢ AQ6
♣ AK102

Bid 2NT, which promises 19-21 HCP. The unusual notrump does not apply in balancing seat because you need 2NT as a natural bid. With 15-18 HCP, double and rebid notrump.

	West	*North*	*East*	*South*
	1◇	P	P	???

♠ K7643
♡ AKJ52
◇ A8
♣ 7

Bid 2◇. Good news, Michaels is still on in balancing seat. With this great hand, you intend to bid on after partner's two-level response.

♠ KJ10643
♡ A8
◇ 53
♣ 853

Bid 1♠. Be careful. The fact that you would prefer to jump to 2♠ to show a weak hand with a six-card suit is not relevant. The balancing jump is strength-showing, so all you can do now is bid at the one level.

♠ A6
♡ 73
◇ A4
♣ AKQ7632

Bid 3NT—what you think you can make. This is the same bid you would have made if your RHO had opened 1◇. If you are concerned about a heart attack, get more exercise.

♠ A3
♡ 8542
◇ 752
♣ A942

Pass. You are neither short in the opponent's suit, nor do you have a good hand. Remember, the only time when partner would pass 1◇ with a good hand is when he has diamond length. If that is the case, defending 1◇ is as good as anything.

♠ AJ105
♡ 84
◇ AKJ
♣ AQJ10

Double. Because you have four spades, do not rush to bid 2NT. You can always do that later after the expected 1♡ response. Players who give themselves extra chances are more likely to get lucky than their less flexible counterparts.

♠ J43
♡ K2
◇ J84
♣ AQ943

Balance with 1NT. In this situation, your lack of a stopper is not an issue. You are expecting partner to have some diamonds because he has values but could not bid. Even if you lose the first four or five tricks, that is no big deal when declaring 1NT.

♠ AJ3
♡ A
◇ 743
♣ KQJ1072

Bid 3♣. The intermediate jump overcall to the three level promises quite a nice hand. I hope that your partnership is on the same wavelength here—disaster waits if partner mistakes this for a weak bid.

♠ KQJ64
♡ A4
◇ A83
♣ K52

Double, planning to bid your spades next, showing the big double. I hope that you would have used the same approach after an opening bid on your right.

Believe it or not, the methods that I have discussed above are considered part of standard bridge. I hope that you agree. Regardless, I recommend that you get together with your favorite partner and discuss your balancing strategy. You will be glad you did.

*   *   *

Speaking of balancing...

A beginner called me over in the middle of some supervised play. The player wanted advice holding 16 HCP and a good six-card suit.

The student said, "I dealt and the bidding has gone:"

West	North	East	South
1♡	P	P	P
2♡	P	P	P

"Is my hand worth bidding three?"

(Contributed by Patrick Jourdain.)

CHAPTER 15
Good Doubles Go a Long Way

The Negative Double Strikes Again

Everyone agrees that it is essential to play negative doubles. Most players also agree to disagree about how they should be played.

I do not expect all (any?) readers to agree with me 100% of the time. I do believe that discussing these auctions is guaranteed to improve partnership understandings.

	West	North	East	South	
♠ A842	1♣	1♠	Dbl	P	♠ 73
♡ A6	1NT	P	2♡	all pass	♡ J87542
◇ 842					◇ AQ6
♣ KQ84					♣ J6

East is not strong enough to bid 2♡ at his first turn, but passing would lack enterprise. He compromises with a negative double, promising four or more hearts and six or more points.

After West's obvious 1NT rebid, it is now time for East to show his heart length. West realizes that East has fewer than ten HCP, and correctly passes. **A negative double followed by a new suit at the two or three level always shows a weak hand**.

	West	North	East	South	
♠ KJ3	1♣	1◇	Dbl	P	♠ Q842
♡ AQ109	2♡	all pass			♡ J864
◇ 73					◇ A62
♣ A764					♣ 82

East does not have much, but with both majors, he is entitled to throw in his two cents at a low level. **The negative double after 1♣ - (1◇) is the one time when responder promises both majors.**

154

West perks up with an invitational jump to 2♡. If you think he went overboard, look at the next two hands that he would have bid 1♡ with:

♠ J73   ♡ K932   ◇ KQJ   ♣ QJ7

♠ K53   ♡ KQ7   ◇ 83   ♣ KJ643

Remember, jumps in response to partner's negative double are not forcing, they are merely encouraging. If West wanted to insist on game with a big hand, he could have jumped to 4♡ or cuebid 2◇.

	West	North	East	South	
♠ A7542	1♠	2♣	Dbl	P	♠ Q8
♡ 64	2◇	P	3NT	all pass	♡ AQ75
◇ AKJ					◇ 8652
♣ 653					♣ AQ2

East is in no hurry to rush to 3NT, which would be a silly contract if West held:

♠ AK743   ♡ KJ104   ◇ 9   ♣ J73

The flexible negative double preserves all his options.

West is not thrilled to be forced to bid over 2♣ doubled. His strong three-card diamond suit looks more biddable than repeating his sketchy spades. Now East can jump to the obvious game.

	West	North	East	South	
♠ A843	1◇	2♣	Dbl	P	♠ 752
♡ A	2♠	P	3◇	all pass	♡ KJ73
◇ Q1082					◇ K7653
♣ Q764					♣ 8

East had been looking forward to responding 1♡. Once North bid 2♣, a 2◇ raise would have been better than passing but that would deny a four-card major. Therefore, he made a negative double.

After 1◇ - (2♣) the negative double promises only one major, not both. Frequently, responder will have interest in a major but be unable to bid the suit at the two level. An analogy that comes to mind here is Stayman. Responder needs only one major to inquire over 1NT.

Once West bids the wrong major, East can retreat to diamonds without any mishap. Better to ask and not receive than never to have asked at all.

	West	North	East	South	
♠ A4	1♣	2◇	Dbl	P	♠ KJ732
♡ A852	3◇	P	3♠	P	♡ QJ107
◇ AK	3NT	P	4♡	all pass	◇ 5
♣ A8753					♣ J42

Any pair that bids this perfectly is ready for the big time. West has a great hand, but it would be wrong to jump to 4♡ at his second turn. East's negative double did not promise hearts. In fact, if spades had been East's only major, 3NT would have been the best contract. West, therefore cuebid to force to game, and awaited developments.

Many players would have passed 3NT with the East cards, but they would be missing an important clue. If all West wanted was to play 3NT, why did he bother to cuebid? The only logical explanation is that he had hearts. East therefore corrects to the best game.

	West	North	East	South	
♠ A4	1◇	2♠	Dbl	P	♠ 863
♡ AJ73	4♡	all pass			♡ K842
◇ AJ8632					◇ Q
♣ 5					♣ A8743

Short and sweet. After East promised hearts, West lost no time jumping to the major-suit game.

	West	North	East	South	
♠ AQ	1◇	3♣	Dbl	P	♠ K842
♡ AK107	4♡	P	5◇	all pass	♡ 64
◇ J8763					◇ AKQ2
♣ 64					♣ 852

We now have an opponent's annoying three-level jump overcall. East's negative double of 3♣ promised at least one major and values, because he was forcing partner to bid at a high level. West had to bid more than 3♡ with his great hearts and reasonable hand so he jumped to 4♡. East corrected to the cold minor-suit game.

	West	North	East	South	
♠ A3	1♡	3◇	Dbl	all pass	♠ 852
♡ K8542					♡ A3
◇ KQJ6					◇ 73
♣ 54					♣ AKJ732

As East, would you have bid 4♣ over 3◇? I think most players would. Here is my suggestion. Play negative doubles at high levels (as opposed to penalty doubles). **However, when the opponent's jump overcall is 3◇ or higher, the double does not guarantee the unbid major(s).** Your number one priority at this level should be to try to get to 3NT.

West was charmed to convert the negative double to penalty with his magnificent diamonds. When the opportunity presents itself, it is fun to "make them pay."

	West	North	East	South	
♠ J53	1♣	3♡	Dbl	P	♠ A4
♡ K6	3NT	all pass			♡ 854
◇ K73					◇ AQJ62
♣ AQ764					♣ K82

Same concept. Try hard to preserve your chances for 3NT.

	West	North	East	South	
♠ AJ	1◇	3♠	Dbl	P	♠ 85
♡ 4	3NT	all pass			♡ K8632
◇ AKQ763					◇ J2
♣ 7642					♣ AK83

Got the message?

Profiting When the Opponents Double

You are East and nobody is vulnerable. The auction proceeds:

West	North	East	South
1♦	Dbl	???	

Do you have anything to tell partner?

♠ 6
♥ KQ743
♦ Q743
♣ K52

Bid 1♥. It would be silly to waste time with a redouble because you want to tell partner about your nice hearts. You will show your points later.

♠ 74
♥ 82
♦ K9532
♣ 8543

Bid 3♦. You have a classic weak jump raise. Although not everyone knows it, it is standard to treat the jump raise as preemptive after the intervening double. The best hands for preempting are those that are short in both majors. You would make the same bid vulnerable.

♠ 73
♥ KJ10953
♦ 83
♣ 742

Bid 2♥—another perfect preempt—you have a good suit and a bad hand. Weak jump shifts in competition should be standard operating procedure.

♠ 74
♥ 8532
♦ K1093
♣ QJ7

Bid 2♦. Although many players would bid 1♥ despite the double, I much prefer 2♦. Partner will know all about your weak hand and diamond support, while the opponents will be unable to look for a spade fit at the one level. Also, if South becomes declarer, you would prefer a diamond lead to any other.

♠ K6
♥ Q83
♦ 743
♣ Q8432

Bid 1NT. Say your piece while it is easy to do so. This bid also serves to push South to the two level.

♠ 873
♥ 84
◇ 842
♣ KQJ109

Bid 2♣, non-forcing. Now here is a suit worth talking about. This bid shows a six-card suit, but that is okay because it looks like one and you are dying to get a club lead.

♠ J832
♥ K72
◇ 8
♣ Q7542

Pass. Yes, you do have six HCP. That means you were obliged to keep the bidding open if RHO had passed. However, now that partner is sure to get another turn to bid, you should speak only if you have something worth saying. With this mess, silence is golden.

♠ 53
♥ KQ109
◇ 742
♣ 8632

Bid 1♥. You will never have a better opportunity to show your lovely hearts. Helping partner choose a lead and getting him off to the right defense are what bridge is all about!

♠ Q106
♥ K5
◇ 82
♣ AQJ764

Bid 3NT. There no doubt that this is where you are headed. Why give the enemy a chance to find a fit (or a lead)? Do not concern yourself with missing a slam, that is very unlikely once the opponents have doubled.

♠ 87532
♥ 7432
◇ —
♣ Q843

Pass. No, you do not want to watch partner declare 1◇ doubled. It will not be pretty! It is unlikely that you are going to play there anyway because LHO will rarely have the overwhelming diamonds he would need to leave in the takeout double.

Even if he does, partner should trust that South's diamonds are better than his and run unless his diamonds are of 24-carat quality. In times like these, last (wo)man runs.

ALERT, new auction:

West	North	East	South
1♠	Dbl	???	

♠ A84
♥ 76
◇ KJ632
♣ Q84

Redouble. You will support spades at your next turn. Partner will then know that you have three spades with 10-12 distributional points. Voilà.

♠ 75
♥ KJ83
◇ KQ732
♣ A4

Again, redouble. You are hoping for blood! You will be delighted to double diamonds or hearts. If partner can double clubs, it is "lights out" for the opponents. If he cannot, you will bid your diamonds (forcing) and go from there.

♠ J843
♥ 7
◇ 87532
♣ 842

Bid 3♠. If jumping to 3♠ with one HCP bothers you, replace the jack with the ten! What if you were vulnerable? Vulnerable, schmulnerable. You have nine trumps, so get your side to the three level quicky, adhering to The LAW.

♠ AJ76
♥ 743
◇ AJ
♣ 8532

Bid 2NT, Jordan. This is a convention I recommend. You are promising four-card support and at least ten points including distribution. If you are not playing Jordan, redouble and then raise spades.

♠ 75
♥ 8643
◇ AQ10743
♣ 6

Bid 2◇. You were delighted to hear the opponent's double. Otherwise, you would have been forced to bid a nondescript 1NT. After the double, a new suit at the two level is not forcing.

After the opponents double partner's opening bid, the rules change. Center stage now goes to competing and preempting. You can throw in your two cents, but with nothing to say, pass for now. "Time is on your side."

Attacking After the Redouble

I am sure that all bridge players have favorite scenarios. Everyone loves to have strong hands and bid slams. Some players cannot wait to double when their opponents step out of line, and some (like me) love to preempt. But I have another favorite which might surprise you.

I love sitting in fourth seat after the bidding has started:

West	North	East	South
1 suit	Dbl	Rdbl	???

"Marty, what is so great about that? Everyone knows that all four players cannot have good hands. Why do you look forward to having nothing?"

That is not it at all. What I love about these auctions is the sense of freedom they provide. After the redouble, fourth hand does not have to bid. If he has nothing to say, he simply passes and waits for his partner to come to the rescue.

Fourth hand can bid whatever he wants (pinch me, I must be dreaming). There are so few points outstanding after the other three players have promised good hands that **all bids by fourth hand promise no strength**. They show distribution, not high cards. For example, after the following...

West	North	East	South
1♡	Dbl	Rdbl	???

...I can bid 1♠ with a hand as weak as:

♠ 10653 ♡ 87643 ◇ 6 ♣ 863

It would be foolish to pass and risk partner's 2◇ rescue attempt with:

♠ AK7 ♡ 92 ◇ J7532 ♣ AQ9

Try the following:

	West	North	East	South
♠ K10965	1♡	Dbl	Rdbl	???
♡ 843				
◇ 9765				
♣ 8				

Once partner promised heart shortness, you know that the opponents have a solid heart fit. Do not make it easy for them to find it. Jump directly to 2♠ (except, of course, if you are playing against me)!

Did I shock you? Is this the kind of bid you could ever get yourself to make? What about vulnerability? Am I really saying that I would make this bid vulnerable?

Yes, I would. Vulnerable, schmulnerable! Let me try to bring you back to earth with a question. What is the risk? Once RHO redoubled, your partner certainly knows that you have a very weak hand. He is not going to hang you. If he does have good support and a distributional hand, a 4♠ sacrifice would be a bargain compared to watching the enemy bid and make 4♡.

The opponents will also know that you have a weak hand. However, they are not going to double you at the two level when your side has eight or nine spades. I know, and play, against the best players in the world. Not one of them is a shrinking violet. However, they know better than to make penalty doubles at low levels unless they have trumps to die for. Failing that, they will overcome your preempt as best as they can, but I guarantee that your 2♠ bid has complicated their lives.

I hope that you are still with me. For those who suspect that I should be committed (editor's note: no comment), here are a few more examples of our "attack mode."

Trump length will be the single most important factor here (remember The Law of Total Tricks). Vulnerability, suit strength and distribution are also important parts of the equation, as is your holding in the opponent's suit. Once partner denies length in the enemy's suit, you can easily evaluate their fit. With neither side vulnerable, we will stay with our favorite auction:

West	North	East	South
1♡	Dbl	Rdbl	???

♠ 7
♡ 75
◊ J87652
♣ 8542

Bid 3◊. Only one HCP? No problem. The weaker you are the more desperate you should be. If you chose 2◊—shame, shame. My second choice was to jump to 4◊.

Notice how we followed The LAW. Partner promised at least three cards in each unbid suit. Our six diamonds, when added to his three, gives us nine. We are always happy to be at the three level with nine trumps.

♠ 54
♡ 73
◇ 9654
♣ KQJ95

Bid 3♣. This should be painless. Although you have five clubs, their strength should reassure any doubting Thomases. Without the redouble, you would have been forced to respond 2♣ after...

West	North	East	South
1♡	Dbl	P	???

...with as little as:

♠ 97   ♡ 7654   ◇ J74   ♣ 9654.

Partner had to be prepared for that when he doubled. Nobody would object to playing one level higher with your actual club holding of KQJ95.

♠ 643
♡ 42
◇ 3
♣ K986532

Bid 4♣. You have no defense, but your side does have ten or eleven clubs. If doubled, you will only need to take eight tricks to better the opponent's score for making 4♡. Not only is that likely, but I would be shocked if the opponents bother to double you in a partscore when they were on their way to 4♡.

Of course, you are hoping that partner has the right hand to sacrifice in 5♣. If you can push the enemy to the five level, you will have created a lovely win-win scenario.

Got the message? Isn't it fun to jump around like this? When you have a sure fit, go for the gusto. Alas, these opportunities do not grow on trees.

You should know that 2NT is natural (11-12 HCP) on this auction:

West	North	East	South
1 major	Dbl	P	2NT

However, after a redouble, it is impossible for South to have 11-12 HCP.

West	North	East	South
1 major	Dbl	Rdbl	2NT

Aha! Let us assign a meaning to this 2NT bid. I call it the "unusual" unusual notrump." As you might expect, it shows the minors. Because partner has promised minor-suit support via his double, you do not have to wait for five-five distribution to use our new toy.

I would happily bid 2NT after...

West	North	East	South
1♡	Dbl	Rdbl	???

...at any vulnerability with either of the following hands because I will be happy to play in partner's better minor at the three level:

♠ 85   ♡ J6   ◇ KJ85   ♣ 108543

♠ 8   ♡ 7542   ◇ K1064   ♣ QJ75

How about 3NT? It is definitely not a natural bid on this auction—how could fourth hand possibly have a good enough hand for that? No, this is also unusual but it shows more distribution. It suggests a five-level sacrifice if partner is shapely. Here is an oldie but a goodie—the enemy was vulnerable.

                              North
                              ♠ A9872
                              ♡ KQ6
                              ◇ J6
                              ♣ 543

West   *East* (Marty)
♠ Q1054   ┌──────────┐   ♠ J
♡ 8   │   5♡   │   ♡ 74
◇ AK942   │ ◇A LEAD │   ◇ Q10753
♣ A102   └──────────┘   ♣ J9876

                              South
                              ♠ K63
                              ♡ AJ109532
                              ◇ 8
                              ♣ KQ

West	North	East	South
—	—	—	1♡
Dbl	Rdbl	3NT	4♡
5◇	5♡	all pass	

5♡ was down one, declarer losing two aces and an eventual spade trick. I would not fault either North or South for their auction; they were only going +100 against 5◇ doubled. If either player had held the ♠10, the 5♡ contract would have come home by taking the spade finesse after East's jack falls.

Now you know why I love this auction. Inexperienced players may wait for good hands, but their experienced counterparts do not. *Points schmoints.*

CHAPTER 16
Declaring Like a Champ

Slow Down, Partner

We all know players who are so excited to be declarer that as soon as dummy is tabled, they are off and running. Unless they are one of the five best players in the world, there is no way they can play effectively in this manner. And even if they are...

My solution? Try the following whenever you partner one of these speed demons. When you become dummy, use this strategy when tabling your hand. Put down your suits in a deliberate manner, one at a time. However, make sure that you **hold back the suit led until last**. Do not be ostentatious about it, but do make sure that your objective is realized.

Why would you do that? To give partner time to look at the entire hand right away. It is amazing how many makable contracts are lost at trick one. In fact, entire books have been devoted to this subject.

I have successfully used this technique with students and experts alike. I cannot guarantee that your partner will become more deliberate as declarer, but I am willing to wager that he does make more of his contracts.

Double Dummy

The highest compliment that can be paid to a player is "he played that hand double dummy." *The Official Encyclopedia of Bridge* defines that as "play of the hand that could not be improved upon, as though declarer were looking at all four hands."

Here is your opportunity to play double dummy. The question is, with all four hands in view, can you make the ridiculous 7♠ doubled contract with the equally idiotic ♡J lead? The solution is provided on the next page. If you succeed, your duplicate score will be +2470. Both sides are vulnerable.

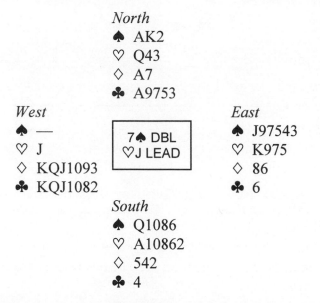

North
♠ AK2
♡ Q43
◇ A7
♣ A9753

West
♠ —
♡ J
◇ KQJ1093
♣ KQJ1082

7♠ DBL
♡J LEAD

East
♠ J97543
♡ K975
◇ 86
♣ 6

South
♠ Q1086
♡ A10862
◇ 542
♣ 4

Do not concern yourself with the auction, no North-South would dream about bidding even a small slam in real life.

Trick 1:   ♡J, Q, K, A (it would not help East to duck).
Trick 2:   ◇2 to dummy's ace (club to the ace is also fine).
Trick 3:   ♡3, 5, 6, West discarding the ◇3.
Trick 4:   ♣4 to dummy's ace.
Trick 5:   ♡4, 7, 8, West discarding the ♣2.
Trick 6:   ♡10, discarding dummy's ◇7, West discarding the ♣8.
Trick 7:   Ruff ◇4 in dummy with the ♠2.
Trick 8:   Lead dummy's ♣3, overruffing East.
Tricks 9-13: Crossruff, overruffing East at tricks 10 and 12.

That will teach the opponents to double you!

*   *   *

Speaking of doubles...

This reminds me of one of my most memorable teaching experiences. Not so long ago, I was teaching a large group of intermediates about doubles. After the lecture, the class began playing the first of my preduplicated lesson hands. Almost immediately, I was called to a table by an obviously agitated player. "My partner just doubled me," she exclaimed. "What do I do now?"

I turned to her very composed partner and asked the obvious question, "Patricia, why did you double your partner?" "Today's subject was doubles, Marty, and you always base your hands on the topic of the day." I chewed that one over while seeking an appropriate yet profound response. However, Patty was far from finished. "The double was easy. My question is: was my double takeout, penalty or negative?"

Four of a Major: The Best Game in Town

Everyone knows that 5♣ and 5◇ are not popular game contracts. I have even heard of teachers telling their students: "You can only play five of a minor if you have a note from your doctor." As to which is better, 3NT or four of a major, some uncertainty remains. I would like to set the record straight with a relevant story.

A study was conducted with the aid of a computer. Thousands of deals were examined, the object being to determine how many tricks would be available on these hands if they were played in different contracts. Of course, we are comparing suit contracts against notrump. Here is a sample.

```
                        North
                        ♠ K73
                        ♡ 1092
                        ◇ K5
                        ♣ KQJ73

        West            ┌─────────┐        East
        ♠ J1095         │   4♡    │        ♠ Q86
        ♡ A53           │ ♠J LEAD │        ♡ 76
        ◇ A1063         └─────────┘        ◇ 9742
        ♣ 54                               ♣ A1098

                        South
                        ♠ A42
                        ♡ KQJ84
                        ◇ QJ8
                        ♣ 62
```

West	North	East	South
—	—	P	1♡
P	2♣	P	2NT
P	4♡	all pass	

North-South bid accurately to their best contract. However, some players holding the North cards would have raised 2NT to 3NT. Not you.

If North-South play in 3NT, they score only eight tricks after a spade lead. The defense cannot be stopped from taking two spades and three aces. Now, examine the play in 4♡, which is more interesting. You appear to have four losers: three aces and a spade. Or do you?

Some declarers would draw trump first, which is wrong. After winning their trump ace, the opponents would continue spades. Now declarer will have four inescapable losers.

A better plan is to develop the club suit. Win the first spade in your hand, saving the ♠K as an entry to dummy. Lead a club from your hand to knock out the ace. After the inevitable spade return, attempt to dispose of your spade loser on dummy's long clubs. No such luck. Because clubs divide four-two (which goes with the odds), West will ruff the third club for the setting trick.

To make the hand, declarer must appreciate that setting up an immediate discard for a losing spade is critical. The diamond suit contains the same three honors as the club suit. Because there are only five diamonds between declarer and dummy (as opposed to seven clubs), the opponents are less likely to ruff that suit. Sometimes shorter is better. Last but not least, declarer must retain an entry to his hand to cash that third diamond.

Proceed as follows: win the spade lead with dummy's king and play the ◇K at trick two. When the opponents win their ◇A, they cannot prevent you from discarding dummy's third spade on your last diamond winner, and ruffing your spade loser in dummy. Very nice, 4♡ bid and made.

After hearing this story, you might anticipate the conclusion of the study. After thousands of deals had been analyzed, the results (after rounding) were: **deals played in an adequate trump suit averaged one and a half tricks more than those played in notrump**.

Our pecking order is clear. Because you can expect an extra one and a half tricks in an adequate trump suit, it must be worthwhile to bid for one additional trick. Therefore, four of a major is superior to 3NT. We now have the definitive answer for North after South rebid 2NT. He should bid 4♡. We also have evidence that explains why 3NT is superior to five of a minor. With only a bonus of one and a half tricks, you cannot justify contracting for two extra tricks to play game in a minor suit rather than 3NT.

Obviously, a few hands will prove to be exceptions. With very flat hands, notrump and suit contracts may produce the same number of tricks. With nine or more trumps and a singleton or void, experience has shown that five of a minor may actually be better than 3NT. However, if you comply with the results of the "one and a half study"...

4 of a major > 3NT > 5 of a minor

...you will not go wrong.

Overtake or Underachieve?

If I were forced to single out the most important topic on cardplay, there is no question what I would choose—entries. How many times have you heard someone lament about how they were "stuck in the wrong hand?"

This often happens when one hand is shorter in a suit than the other and the "short" hand has higher cards than the "long" hand. In this case, special measures may be called for.

The following hand is just such a case. "How could you play your ace on my king?" exclaimed the amazed dummy on the following hand. "Trust me," stated declarer, "I have a good plan." Indeed he did.

```
                      North
                      ♠ A432
                      ♡ K
                      ◇ AQJ
                      ♣ AQ653
      West                              East
      ♠ KQJ9         ┌──────────┐       ♠ 108
      ♡ 754          │   3NT    │       ♡ Q632
      ◇ 9862         │ ♠K LEAD  │       ◇ 543
      ♣ J8           └──────────┘       ♣ K1092
                      South
                      ♠ 765
                      ♡ AJ1098
                      ◇ K107
                      ♣ 74
```

West	North	East	South
—	1♣	P	1♡
P	2♠	P	2NT
P	3NT	all pass	

West had an obvious spade lead, even though North had bid the suit. Although there are exceptions to almost everything, I have strong feelings about sequence leads. When I am on lead and have a sequence in a suit I usually think, "Thank you, Lord" for solving my opening lead problem.

Declarer allowed West to win the first trick with the king of spades. Declarer won the second trick with his ace. He could only count seven winners: one spade, one club, two hearts and three diamonds. How should he proceed to guarantee the contract?

Declarer led the ♡K and overtook it with his ace, causing his partner to gasp. However, it was now easy to set up his hearts by forcing out the queen; the ♢K still remained as the vital entry.

It was crucial for declarer to overtake the ♡K. If he had not, he would have had only one entry to his hand—the ♢K. Two entries were needed; one to knock out the queen and the other to reenter his hand to enjoy the established heart winners. No other plan would have succeeded.

"Well played," North exclaimed after 3NT rolled home. "Would you like to play again?" You must admit—this dummy was no dummy.

Entries—the Name of the Game

Here is a little play problem for you. Note the title of this article and decide how you would proceed as declarer before reading on. West leads the ♠7 against 3NT. East will play the ♠3 to the first trick.

North
♠ KJ5
♡ J10873
◇ 643
♣ 83

```
┌──────────────┐
│    3NT       │
│  ♠7 LEAD     │
└──────────────┘
```

South
♠ A92
♡ Q9
◇ AKJ5
♣ AK42

West	North	East	South
—	—	—	2NT
P	3◇*	P	3♡
P	3NT	all pass	

* Alerted as a transfer to hearts.

Did you win the first trick in dummy with the ♠J? For shame. It would also be wrong to win the trick cheaply with your ♠9.

Declarer must win the first trick with his ♠A in order to preserve two entries to dummy's hearts. This is safe because West is marked with the ♠Q based on The Rule of 11. When a fourth-best lead is made, subtract the card led from 11. The difference represents the number of higher cards held by the other three players (excluding the opening leader). Because declarer is looking at four higher spades (dummy's king-jack and his ace-nine) he is 100% sure that East has no spade above the seven.

Now declarer is home free. East should duck South's ♡Q at trick two but declarer can continue hearts and overtake his ♡9 with dummy's ♡10, driving out a heart honor. Whatever East returns, South can win and use dummy's two spade entries to set up and run hearts. Declarer will win ten tricks: three in each major and two in each minor.

The full deal:

North
♠ KJ5
♡ J10873
◇ 643
♣ 83

West
♠ Q1087
♡ 54
◇ Q987
♣ Q75

```
3NT
♠7 LEAD
```

East
♠ 643
♡ AK62
◇ 102
♣ J1096

South
♠ A92
♡ Q9
◇ AKJ5
♣ AK42

Winners Take Care of Their Losers

Have I got a hand for you!

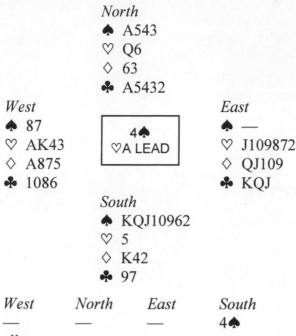

```
                      North
                      ♠ A543
                      ♡ Q6
                      ◇ 63
                      ♣ A5432
West                  ┌──────────┐        East
♠ 87                  │    4♠    │        ♠ —
♡ AK43                │ ♡A LEAD  │        ♡ J109872
◇ A875                └──────────┘        ◇ QJ109
♣ 1086                                    ♣ KQJ
                      South
                      ♠ KQJ10962
                      ♡ 5
                      ◇ K42
                      ♣ 97
```

West	North	East	South
—	—	—	4♠

all pass

Nice dummy! Your decision to open 4♠ worked like a charm; the opponents can probably make more than you. It would be even better if you can score this up. Any player can make the hand if East has the ◇A, but good players make their own luck. Can you see any hope if the ◇A is offside?

West leads the ♡A and follows with the king at trick two. The spotlight is on you. Choose your line of play before reading on.

If you ruff the ♡K, you will be unable to make the hand even though clubs divide three-three. Any attempt to set them up will result in two fast diamond losers. When East gets in with his club winner, he will shift to the ◇Q. Therefore, you must discard your inevitable club loser on West's ♡K at trick two. Now you can hope to establish dummy's clubs, but in order to enjoy them, you will have to get to the table three times. The two aces are the obvious choices, but where is your third entry? If you remember to save your teeny spade deuce now, it will become very big later. Play as follows:

Assume that West punts by playing a trump at trick three (which is as good as anything).

Trick 3:   Win the ♠K in your hand.
Trick 4:   Cash your ♠Q, drawing West's last trump.
Trick 5:   Lead a club to dummy's ace.
Trick 6:   Trump a club with your ♠J.
Trick 7:   Lead the ♠2 to dummy's remaining low card (an artist would have preserved dummy's three, but take full credit for either the four or five).
Trick 8:   Trump another club. When clubs split, you are home.
Trick 9:   Lead a spade to dummy's ace.
Trick 10: Cash dummy's ♣4, discarding a diamond from your hand.
Trick 11: Cash dummy's ♣5, getting rid of another nasty diamond.

With two cards left, concede a diamond and claim.

What would you have done if clubs had not split? Then and only then would you have shrugged your shoulders and taken the diamond finesse. When that lost, you would have been justified in lamenting your bad luck. Of course, since East-West is cold for a heart slam, you still have no regrets.

The technique used here is referred to as the "loser on loser" play. It can be defined as: declarer's choice not to trump, preferring instead to discard an inevitable side-suit loser.

Back in 1976, my first bridge student was a gentleman who was addicted to this strategy. He had read about a declarer who had successfully employed it, and he believed that virtually all hands should be played that way.

Unfortunately, his passion exceeded his ability. In fact, he took this play to a totally new level. On many hands, Fred would throw "winners on losers."

Lose Early—Win Often

Good players do not mind giving up a few tricks if they will gain more than they lose in the process. Unfortunately, this principle is sometimes difficult to apply at the table. On the following deal, I was playing with an experienced Life Master who had won his share of tournaments. I became dummy and watched as partner took a line of play that—well—could have been better. He was in such a hurry to get rid of his one club loser that he failed to even consider what to do with all his diamonds.

North (Marty)
♠ AK6
♡ A10953
◇ 5
♣ 9643

West
♠ 1032
♡ 872
◇ A109
♣ KQJ8

```
┌─────────────┐
│    4♠       │
│  ♣K LEAD    │
└─────────────┘
```

East
♠ 87
♡ QJ64
◇ KQ62
♣ 1052

South
♠ QJ954
♡ K
◇ J8743
♣ A7

West	North	East	South
—	1♡	P	1♠
P	2♠	P	4♠

The raise to 2♠ would not be everyone's choice, but AK6 in partner's major looks awfully good to me. Anyway, on to the play.

Declarer could not wait to get rid of his losing club. He won the ♣A and cashed his ♡K. He immediately crossed to dummy's ♠A and cashed the ♡A, triumphantly discarding his club loser. He now continued with the ◇5, creating a void in dummy. West won the diamond with his nine, and it was obvious to him to lead trumps. In fact, West now wished that he had led a trump at trick one. Declarer won the trump return in his hand and ruffed a diamond with dummy's last trump.

Here was the position with North on lead at trick eight:

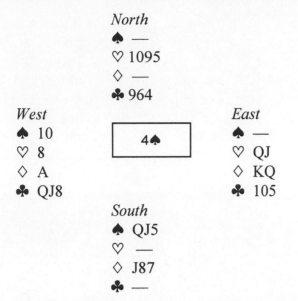

North
♠ —
♡ 1095
◇ —
♣ 964

West
♠ 10
♡ 8
◇ A
♣ QJ8

4♠

East
♠ —
♡ QJ
◇ KQ
♣ 105

South
♠ QJ5
♡ —
◇ J87
♣ —

Although declarer had not lost any tricks in clubs or hearts, dummy's diamond void was worthless because he was also out of trumps. Each time declarer led diamonds, the defenders returned clubs or hearts, forcing declarer to ruff. He eventually ran out of trumps and lost control of the hand, finishing down one.

Declarer should have spent his energy seizing an opportunity. After all, the opponents had not led trumps and he was free to set up a crossruff. He should also have counted winners as follows: two hearts and the ♣A represent three tricks in the side suits. Five trump winners in my hand brings the total to eight. Two ruffs in dummy? No problem.

Lead a diamond at trick two. West wins and should shift to a trump. It would be wrong for West to attempt to cash a club because declarer might be void. Rather, he must remove a trump from each of the North-South hands.

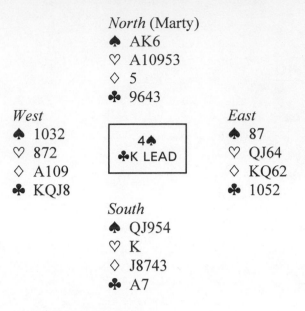

North (Marty)
- ♠ AK6
- ♡ A10953
- ◇ 5
- ♣ 9643

West
- ♠ 1032
- ♡ 872
- ◇ A109
- ♣ KQJ8

4♠
♣K LEAD

East
- ♠ 87
- ♡ QJ64
- ◇ KQ62
- ♣ 1052

South
- ♠ QJ954
- ♡ K
- ◇ J8743
- ♣ A7

The play continues as follows:

Trick 3: Win West's trump shift with the ace.
Trick 4: Lead a heart to the king.
Trick 5: Trump a diamond with the ♠6 in dummy.
Trick 6: Cash the ♡A, discarding a club from hand.
Trick 7: Trump a club with your ♠5.
Trick 8: Trump a diamond with dummy's ♠K.
Trick 9: Trump a club with your ♠9.

Declarer has now won eight tricks and is still sitting pretty with the QJ of trumps for two more. He has ten winners, making 4♠.

This hand was played in a team match, and I expected a considerable loss unless our teammates found a trump opening lead. What happened? Bad news, good news. Our teammates also led from their strong club holding against 4♠, and the experienced declarer at their table played the hand exactly the same way as my partner had.

Too bad I was not playing with you!

CHAPTER 17
Did You Get My Message?

My Kingdom for a Signal

There are three basic defensive signals: attitude, count and suit preference. We will examine them individually.

*   *   *

The **attitude signal** is used to tell partner whether or not you like the suit he led. To give an attitude signal, play a high card to encourage partner, a low one to discourage. It is critical, however, that you **never signal with a card that might represent a potential winner.**

The attitude signal is used when partner leads a suit and you are not involved in competing for the trick. It is also used when you are discarding, regardless of who led the suit.

*   *   *

Count is used to tell partner whether you have an odd or even number of cards in the suit declarer led. A high card shows an even number (again, do not waste a high card that might become a winner) and a low card shows an odd number.

*   *   *

Suit preference is used to ask partner to lead a specific suit. A play of a high card asks for the lead of the higher-ranking of the other two suits. A low card asks for the lead of the lower-ranking suit.

The primary use of suit preference is when giving, or attempting to give, a ruff. It can be used when dummy has a singleton and third hand is not competing for the trick. This signal is also useful if you are setting up your suit in a notrump contract. When you knock out the enemy's last stopper, the card you play in your suit is a suit-preference signal. There are other rare, advanced situations when logic dictates use of suit preference. These occur when partner needs to find your strength. Happy signaling!

179

Counting on Partner's Count

Every player realizes the need to tell partner about his hand during the bidding. However, communication during the play of the hand— specifically on defense—receives far less attention. This is unfortunate because defense is the most difficult part of the game.

Everyone knows about attitude signals. A high card indicates a good holding, suggesting that partner continue the suit. However, what many players do not realize is that **attitude signals are given only when partner leads a suit, or when discarding** no matter who leads the suit. **When declarer's side leads a suit, the appropriate signal to give is count**.

The good news is that count signals are much easier to give than attitude signals. And there is no bad news! It is just a question of getting accustomed to them and remembering when they apply.

Here is the scoop: when declarer leads a side suit from either hand, the defenders should give count. When competing for the trick, you will not be able to signal. However, as soon as you get the chance, proceed as follows:

How do you signal with a doubleton? High, then low. What kind of number is two? An even number—just like four, six and eight. NOTE: if you are on defense holding an eight-card suit, we need to have a chat. With an even number of cards, play the highest you can afford. With an odd number of cards, play your lowest one first.

That is all there is to it!

How does partner react to your signal? First, he must train himself to notice your card! All the great signals in the world are worthless if partner is not paying attention.

I hope that you are fortunate enough to have an observant partner, which is often not the case. The following is precisely what should happen when declarer's side leads the suit and partner gives count:

1. You add dummy's number of cards to your own, and subtract from 13. The difference is the total held by declarer and partner.

2. You notice and memorize partner's card.

3. You analyze partner's card and, based on what you see, decide whether it is high or low. You now know whether partner began with an odd or even number. Subtract to get an idea of declarer's holding.

4. You try to figure out the exact distribution of the concealed hands, relying on bridge logic and clues from the bidding.

5. You take appropriate action.

Overwhelmed? Do not despair, a few examples will prove to be worth many words! Take a look at this one. You are East.

North
♡ QJ105

West
♡ 2

East (You)
♡ A7643

South
♡ K

Declarer opens 1NT, which ends the auction. After your partner leads another suit, declarer wins and attacks hearts. Tell me about the distribution of the heart suit.

Step 1   You see a total of nine cards between dummy and your hand. Declarer and partner began with a total of four (13-9) cards.

Step 2   You observe partner's deuce.

Step 3   Because partner's card is low, he must have an odd number: one or three. Therefore, declarer also has one or three.

Step 4   Declarer opened 1NT; he cannot hold the singleton. Partner must hold the singleton, leaving declarer with exactly three hearts.

Step 5   You intend to hold up your ace until the third round. Why? A cardinal principle for the defenders when declarer is attempting to establish dummy's suit: **wait until the short hand is playing its last card in the suit before you take your winner**.

With a different auction, you would not have known who had the singleton. Fortunately, there are often clues available from the bidding and/or the play. For example, if the hand had been played in a suit contract, you would reason: if partner held a singleton, he would have led it.

Now make a slight change from the previous layout:

North
♡ QJ105

West   *East*
♡ 9   ♡ A72

South
♡ K

Again, assume South's 1NT opening was passed out.

Step 1   There are seven hearts between your hand and dummy's. The other two players have a total of six hearts.

Step 2   Memorize partner's nine.

Step 3   When partner signals with the nine, he has an even number of cards in the suit (unless he holds the singleton nine). You already know that there are six outstanding hearts, so partner holds either two or four of them. Therefore, declarer must have two or four.

You do not yet know the exact distribution, so play low and bide your time.

Steps 4-5 If declarer began with two hearts, you need to take your ace the second time the suit is played. If declarer began with four, you cannot prevent him from winning three tricks in the suit. Therefore, you should assume that declarer has two.

Here is a deal where giving and receiving count is crucial:

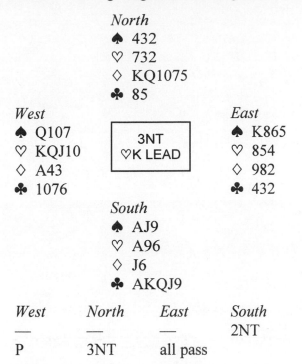

North
♠ 432
♡ 732
♢ KQ1075
♣ 85

West
♠ Q107
♡ KQJ10
♢ A43
♣ 1076

3NT
♡K LEAD

East
♠ K865
♡ 854
♢ 982
♣ 432

South
♠ AJ9
♡ A96
♢ J6
♣ AKQJ9

West	North	East	South
—	—	—	2NT
P	3NT	all pass	

The bidding was short and sweet. A 2NT opening with 20-21 HCP is fairly standard for experienced players.

Declarer held up his ♡A until the third round. Instead of running clubs, which would help the defenders, he went to work on dummy's diamonds. He hoped that his opponents would instinctively hold up their ace until the third time the suit was played. South would then run for cover and unleash his club surprise, taking five clubs, two diamonds and the two aces for nine tricks.

Unfortunately for declarer, East-West were a good pair who rely on count instead of instinct. West could see eight diamonds between his hand and dummy's, which left five for the other two players. West trusted partner's ♢2, promising an odd number. He knew that South started with two or four diamonds, but not three. If South started with four, no holdup would exhaust declarer. Therefore, West assumed that South held two diamonds, and was careful to win the second trick in that suit.

Notice what would have happened if South had held a third diamond instead of a fifth club.

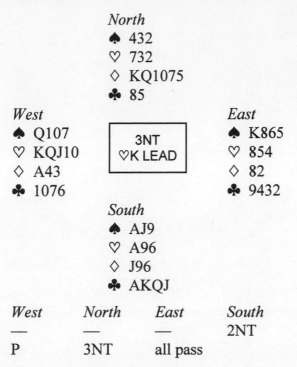

North
♠ 432
♡ 732
◇ KQ1075
♣ 85

West
♠ Q107
♡ KQJ10
◇ A43
♣ 1076

3NT
♡K LEAD

East
♠ K865
♡ 854
◇ 82
♣ 9432

South
♠ AJ9
♡ A96
◇ J96
♣ AKQJ

West	North	East	South
—	—	—	2NT
P	3NT	all pass	

All I did was exchange South's ♣9 for East's ◇9. Now it would be fatal for West to grab the second diamond; South would still have a diamond to lead to dummy. Now, East's first diamond play will be the eight, so once again, West will know what to do.

If your partner has not been defending too well, is it possible that your signals have been more offensive than defensive?

Scintillating Communication

"To have learned to play a good game of bridge is the safest insurance against the tedium of old age."

Somerset Maugham

Poor Jane. Not only was she dealt another Yarborough, but it bore a striking similarity to a recent hand. "Deja vu," thought Jane, gazing at:

♠ 76   ♡ 86543   ◇ 2   ♣ 97642

"Oh well, I have been playing a lot of bridge lately. It feels like a good time for a little R&R."

"Oh, the bidding is over already. Is it my lead? I would love to lead my singleton. But no, I'm not on lead. Okay, back to sleep."

North
♠ AKQJ
♡ AKQJ9
◇ Q5
♣ J10

West		*East* (Jane)
♠ 542	┌─────────┐	♠ 76
♡ —	│ 4♠ │	♡ 86543
◇ AKJ1083	│ ◇K LEAD │	◇ 2
♣ A853	└─────────┘	♣ 97642

South
♠ 10983
♡ 1072
◇ 9764
♣ KQ

West	*North*	*East*	*South*
1◇	Dbl	P	1♠
2◇	4♠	all pass	

"Wow, what a dummy, although it also looks familiar! 23 HCP. They must be making this. Let's get it over with. Wait a moment, how could partner lead the ◇K when dummy has the queen? We lead ace from ace-king. Partner would only lead the king from AK with a doubleton. That's impossible once she bid diamonds. I guess that she forgot. It happens to the best of us!"

(hand repeated for convenience)

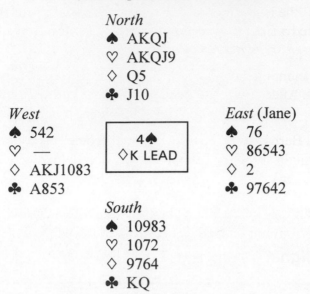

North
- ♠ AKQJ
- ♡ AKQJ9
- ◇ Q5
- ♣ J10

West
- ♠ 542
- ♡ —
- ◇ AKJ1083
- ♣ A853

4♠
◇K LEAD

East (Jane)
- ♠ 76
- ♡ 86543
- ◇ 2
- ♣ 97642

South
- ♠ 10983
- ♡ 1072
- ◇ 9764
- ♣ KQ

"Now if that wasn't strange enough, she plays the ♣A at trick two. That's an interesting lead. I know that we don't lead ace from ace-king after trick one. Am I dreaming? Well, whatever partner is doing, I don't like clubs. Here's a two."

"The ◇A, our third trick, time for a discard. I don't have anything to tell her, although by now I'm so confused that I will probably mess it up anyway. Barbara usually plays so carefully and thoughtfully. What is going on? I should try to give her some information. I already told her about clubs. What else is there?"

"Jane, it's your turn to play." Declarer's words invaded her thoughts.

"Wait a moment. Wake up Janie! I've been so busy thinking about myself. What about Barbara? By making an odd lead, she must be trying to tell me something! I better trust her. What could be so important to justify the 'wrong' lead? Think, Janie, think! Gee, I have a really bad hand here and I still have to think."

"That's it! She has a void. She is trying to tell me that she can trump something if I get the lead. And I can! Could she be void in clubs now? No, she would have led a singleton ♣A at trick one. Therefore, she must have a heart void!"

Jane calmly trumped the ◇A. Both her opponents looked at her as if she had lost her mind. After Jane returned a heart for her to ruff, Barbara beamed. Down one.

Do Jane and Barbara play better than most people? Absolutely. On the other hand, you might surprise yourself if you do the following. Pay attention on every hand, never give up, and most of all, trust your partner.

*   *   *

A Ten-Cent Signal With a Five-Cent Partner

A bridge teacher has just taught her beginners the attitude signal: a high card indicates that "you like the suit."

Defending 5♣ on the first hand, the opening leader correctly led the ◇A from ◇AK64. Partner alertly signaled with the nine. The king was led at the second trick, and partner followed with the two. However, at trick three, diamonds were abandoned, after which declarer took the rest of the tricks.

The teacher asked the opening leader: "Didn't your partner's nine tell you he liked the lead, and wanted you to continue the suit?"

"Well, yes, but when he played the two, I thought he must have changed his mind."

CHAPTER 18
Passing the Defensive Test

A Good Uppercut is Hard to Find

You are West, looking at a terrific hand. You are getting ready to do some serious bidding when South opens 3♠. That is kind of annoying, but no choice, you bid the obvious 4♡. The auction continues with 4♠ by LHO, back around to you. Should you double? Probably not. Should you bid at the five level all by yourself. No, that is crazy. So you pass.

It is your lead. How about your singleton. No, that is unilateral. You make the normal lead of the ♡A.

Partner signals with the ♡7. You continue with your ♡K and everyone follows, partner playing the deuce.

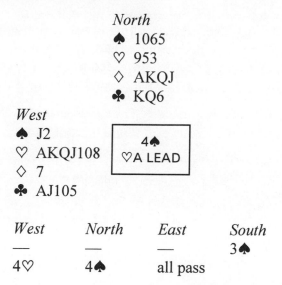

```
                        North
                        ♠ 1065
                        ♡ 953
                        ◇ AKQJ
                        ♣ KQ6
        West
        ♠ J2            ┌─────────┐
        ♡ AKQJ108       │   4♠    │
        ◇ 7             │ ♡A LEAD │
        ♣ AJ105         └─────────┘
```

West	North	East	South
—	—	—	3♠
4♡	4♠	all pass	

How do you defend? Think about where you will find the setting trick.

Here is the entire hand. How did you do?

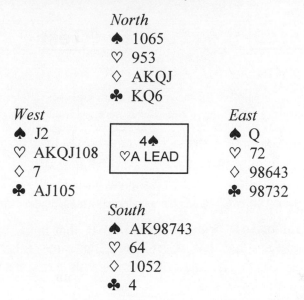

North
- ♠ 1065
- ♡ 953
- ◇ AKQJ
- ♣ KQ6

West
- ♠ J2
- ♡ AKQJ108
- ◇ 7
- ♣ AJ105

4♠
♡A LEAD

East
- ♠ Q
- ♡ 72
- ◇ 98643
- ♣ 98732

South
- ♠ AK98743
- ♡ 64
- ◇ 1052
- ♣ 4

The winning defense is for West to cash the ♣A immediately and continue with the ♡8. It would be wrong for him to lead a heart honor, this would tell East not to ruff. Leading your lowest heart will make it obvious for partner to ruff with his ♠Q. Declarer will be forced to overruff, promoting your ♠J for the setting trick. This elegant play is called an uppercut.

It was crucial to cash the ♣A first. Suppose you led the ♡8 at trick three. When partner correctly ruffed with his ♠Q, declarer would discard his club loser and easily win all the remaining tricks.

I am sure you now agree that on defense, timing is everything.

Some Instincts are Better Than Others

Many players prefer to rely on their instincts rather than force themselves to think. While this approach is sensible in fast-paced sports like racquetball or hockey, it is not recommended in games of logic such as bridge and chess.

Although an expert's instincts may be exceptional, they are not perfect. Every expert knows that when he plays without thinking, he pays for it.

If that is true for experts, imagine what happens to the average player. Unfortunately, it has been my experience that most players rely upon their dubious instincts for far too many of their decisions.

When it comes to defense, relying on instincts is totally inadequate. There is just too much that can be figured out only by logical thought. On the deal we are about to study, East has several decisions to make after winning the first trick. The contract is 4♡ and East-West is vulnerable. Partner leads the ♠2 which you win. Now what?

```
                      North
                      ♠ KQ106
                      ♡ QJ9
                      ◇ 3
                      ♣ AJ1065
      West                              East
      ♠ 2            ┌──────────┐       ♠ A98543
      ♡ 74           │   4♡     │       ♡ A2
      ◇ J10862       │ ♠2 LEAD  │       ◇ KQ97
      ♣ 98432        └──────────┘       ♣ 7
                      South
                      ♠ J7
                      ♡ K108653
                      ◇ A54
                      ♣ KQ
```

West	North	East	South
—	—	1♠	2♡
P	4♡	all pass	

On the first trick, the ♠6 was played from dummy, East won his ace and declarer dropped the jack. This intelligent falsecard might have deceived a sleeping defender, but East had his thinking cap on (for now).

East counted ten spades between his own hand and dummy's, leaving only three for the other two players. If South's jack had been a singleton, West would have been dealt two spades. The lead of the two eliminated that possibility. Everybody knows to lead high from a doubleton, and one thing that you can say about twos, they are never high. Therefore, West had to be the player with the singleton, and South was the comedian.

East was very pleased with himself for his successful reasoning. However, all this thinking must have taken a lot out of him. He could not wait to follow his instincts, so he returned the ♠3 for partner to ruff.

Unfortunately, the only other trick for the defense was the ♡A. South pulled trumps after winning West's club return and ruffed high when spades were continued. Declarer then drew the last trump and won the rest of the tricks to score up his game. East had missed out on a golden opportunity.

Four tricks had been needed to defeat the 4♡ contract—one spade ruff plus two aces would not be enough. Before putting West on lead for the last time, East had to void himself of clubs. Then, with a defensive crossruff in place, declarer would have been helpless. He could try to pull trumps, but East would hop up with the trump ace and give partner his spade ruff. West would then return a club for the setting trick.

Your instincts would suggest giving partner a ruff any time he is void. As you can see from this deal, even that cannot be taken for granted. Next time, leave your instincts at home and try the thinking person's approach. You just might surprise yourself.

On the next deal, West had a chance to shine.

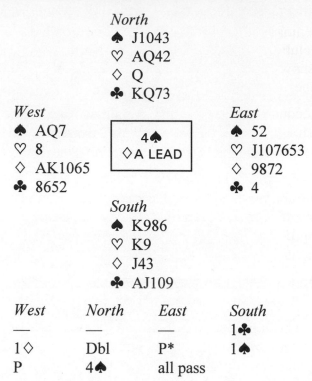

North
♠ J1043
♡ AQ42
◇ Q
♣ KQ73

West
♠ AQ7
♡ 8
◇ AK1065
♣ 8652

4♠
◇ A LEAD

East
♠ 52
♡ J107653
◇ 9872
♣ 4

South
♠ K986
♡ K9
◇ J43
♣ AJ109

West	North	East	South
—	—	—	1♣
1◇	Dbl	P*	1♠
P	4♠	all pass	

The double was negative.
* I would have made a weak jump raise to 3 ◇.

West had a choice of attractive opening leads and selected the more flexible diamond. He was now able to retain the lead while taking a look at dummy. This gave him time to decide whether to continue diamonds or try for a heart ruff. After seeing dummy's singleton diamond, West lost no time playing a heart. Unfortunately for the defense, East never obtained the lead and declarer was smart enough not to play hearts again.

Declarer won the heart shift on the board in order to finesse for the ♠ Q. The ♠J lost to the queen, but declarer was in control. West actually continued by leading ace and another spade, hoping to cut down on diamond ruffs in dummy. Declarer had no trouble with his two remaining diamond losers. He ruffed one and discarded the other on the ♡Q.

After the opening lead of the ♢A, West's instinctive heart shift was a waste of time. With 27 HCP in view between West and North, South needed the ♡K for his opening bid. So instead of leading his singleton, West should have counted the club suit. West had four, as did North. South had opened 1♣, which often shows four cards. If South had been dealt those four, East could only have one.

There was a second clue available. When dummy holds a singleton in a side suit, giving an attitude signal is impractical. Good players give suit-preference signals in this situation. Therefore, East's ♢2 suggested that West return the lower-ranking suit, clubs.

If West had shifted to a club at trick two, South would have been history. He would have won the club and played trumps. West would win and lead a second club, giving East a ruff for the third defensive trick. The ♠A would suffice to set the contract.

When defending against a suit contract, most players' instincts tell them to lead a singleton whenever they hold one. Unless there is a realistic chance that your partner can gain the lead, what is the point?

Ask yourself, "Are you a thoughtful player, or are you content to 'throw cards' and hope for the best?"

A Shift in Time

Up for a little challenge? Try your skills on this one:

> *North*
> ♠ KQ
> ♡ J764
> ◇ AJ9
> ♣ AKJ9

```
┌──────────────┐
│     4♡       │
│  ♠J LEAD     │
└──────────────┘
```

East
♠ A876
♡ 98
◇ Q102
♣ 7642

West	North	East	South
—	1♣	P	1♡
P	4♡	all pass	

You are East, and you win the first trick with your ♠A. What would you lead at trick two?

> *North*
> ♠ KQ
> ♡ J764
> ◇ AJ9
> ♣ AKJ9

West
♠ J10952
♡ K5
◇ K863
♣ 53

```
┌──────────────┐
│     4♡       │
│  ♠J LEAD     │
└──────────────┘
```

East
♠ A876
♡ 98
◇ Q102
♣ 7642

South
♠ 43
♡ AQ1032
◇ 754
♣ Q108

When I use this hand in my classes, most players make the passive return of a spade or heart. While passive defense is sometimes best, the combination of dummy's strong clubs and your very small ones should help point you towards the winning defense.

Notice what will happen after a passive return. Declarer will draw trumps by finessing for the king. Regardless of what partner returns when he gets in with the ♥K, South can draw trumps and discard one of his diamond losers on dummy's clubs.

The only winning shift at trick two is the ◇2. Once partner's king forces out dummy's ace, the defense is in control. When partner gains the lead with his ♥K, he will happily return your suit and your two diamond winners will defeat the contract.

Too many players' defensive thoughts are preoccupied with slogans from their past. "Right, light," "cover an honor with an honor," "second hand low," "don't finesse your partner," etc. These may be helpful for beginners, but aspiring players must strive to understand the unique nature of every new bridge hand and remember to think.

* * *

Dear Marty: My bridge teacher has told me repeatedly about leading the top card from a sequence. I played in a duplicate recently with this teacher and picked up:

♠ KJ97 ♥ J43 ◇ 63 ♣ QJ108

The auction proceeded as follows:

West	North	East	South
1♠	P	1NT	P
2◇	all pass		

I proudly led the ♣Q. Would you believe it, my teacher said that I should have led a trump. What a hypocrite! Should I look elsewhere for lessons?

Misled in Hackensack

Dear Misled: NO! Do not even think of straying. Your teacher is an absolute treasure. Although I too love sequence leads, a trump lead is a standout on this auction. Dummy must be short in spades, and declarer will be eager to ruff his spade losers. The only better lead than a trump would be two trumps!

The Defense Rests (But They Should Have Stayed Awake)

North
♠ KJ10
♡ Q1098
♢ KJ64
♣ QJ

West
♠ 954
♡ 6542
♢ 8
♣ A7643

3NT
♣4 LEAD

East
♠ 8732
♡ AKJ
♢ 732
♣ K98

South
♠ AQ6
♡ 73
♢ AQ1095
♣ 1052

West	North	East	South
—	—	—	1♢
P	1♡	P	1NT
P	3NT	all pass	

Trick 1:   Club to the king.
Trick 2:   ♣9 ducked to dummy's queen.

Declarer now claimed nine tricks.

Obviously, the defense could have taken two clubs and three heart tricks. When the smoke cleared, East blamed West, and West blamed East. I have some strong opinions here (what else is new?) but first I will give you the opportunity to play judge and jury. What do you believe went wrong?

Most players blame West. I am positive that very few players would duck their ♣A at trick two. Of course, even if West had won the ♣A, I cannot imagine any logic that would dictate a heart shift.

Actually, I have nothing but praise for West's defense. From his point of view, clubs offered the only chance to beat the hand. He knew from partner's intelligent ♣9 that declarer's ♣10 entitled him to one trick. West could have won the ♣A and knocked out declarer's ten, but that would have been an exercise in futility. Setting up two club winners when West had no semblance of an entry could not accomplish anything.

West hoped that East had started with three clubs. By giving declarer his inevitable club trick while preserving his ace, West would be able to run clubs as soon as East gained the lead. East was marked with points—it was just unlucky that declarer had nine fast tricks.

Actually, East was well-placed to know everything. He knew that all he needed was a heart shift from West to defeat the contract. The handwriting was on the wall—too bad East could not read it.

After winning the ♣K, East should have first led the ♡K (remember, only lead the ace from ace-king on opening lead). Then, and only then, should he return partner's club lead. After that start, I bet that West would have been delighted to grab his ♣A and return partner's heart lead.

Moral of the story? When you know what is best, make sure to let your partner in on the secret, loud and clear. After all, it is no fun to know a secret if nobody else knows that you know it.

CHAPTER 19
The Lighter Side

Time for Trivia

Here are 13 questions. Answers are on the next page (no peeking).

1. What distribution of 13 cards occurs most often in bridge?

2. What is the most number of points you can lose on a single hand?

3. What are the pointed suits?

4. What card mesmerized Lawrence Harvey throughout the movie *The Manchurian Candidate*?

5. What famous athlete would have been an impressive bidder? (Hint: he had forelegs.)

6. True or false? All doubles are unlimited in strength.

7. There are two solved bridge murders on record. How many of the murderers were male?

8. *Chicane* is a:
   a) tricky play   b) passed-out hand   c) void
   d) hand dealt after the previous one was passed out

9. Name the following, both of whom preferred major suits:
   a) A fictional detective who never worried about being outbid.
   b) A politician who failed to obtain the Democratic nomination.

10. What was Charles Goren's profession before turning to bridge?

11. What is the rabbi's rule?

12. What playing card did Charlie Brown once compare himself to while feeling blue?

13. Would you prefer to declare 3NT if your side's HCP were split 13-13, or would you rather have 20 in your hand and six in dummy?

And now, the answers:

1. Two four-card suits and 3-2 in the other two (4-4-3-2).

2. 7600! Down 13, redoubled, vulnerable.

3. Spades and diamonds, the suits with "points" ♠ and ◇.

4. ◇Q.

5. Spectacular Bid.

6. True (well, almost true, you can only have 37 HCP in one hand).

7. Zero. The only two players charged with committing murder at the bridge table were women.

8. C (void).

9. a) Sam Spade. b) Gary Hart.

10. Attorney.

11. "When the king is singleton, play the ace."

12. ♣2.

13. No comparison. For communication purposes, 13 points in each hand is much better.

*   *   *

Competing With Myself

My student Arlene asked me if I would give a few private lessons to her mother for a Chanukah present. I was happy to do so and told her to have her mother call me when the time was right.

I never heard anything further from either of them. One day in class, I asked Arlene if her mother was ready to begin.

"Oh, I meant to tell you. I gave my mother a copy of *Points Schmoints!* a few weeks ago, and now she says that she no longer needs any lessons!"

For Bridge Players Only

A house maid was applying for a new position, and when asked why she left her last employment, she replied:

Yes sir, they paid good wages, but it was
the strangest place I ever worked for.
They played a game called Bridge and
last night a lot of folks were there.
As I was about to bring in the refreshments,
I hear a man say,
"Lay down and let's see what you've got."
Another man says,
"I got the strength but no length..."
And another man says to a lady:
"Take your hands off my trick."
I pretty near drop dead just then, when a lady
answered: "You forced me. You jumped me twice
when you didn't have the strength for a raise."
Another lady was talking about protecting her honor,
and two other ladies were talking and saying:
"Now it's time for me to play with your husband
and you can play with mine."
Well, I just got my hat and coat and was leaving.
I hope to die if one of them didn't say:
"I guess we'll go home soon.
This is my last rubber."

The Trouble With Doubles
By Steve Becker (© King Features Syndicate)

Twas the night before Christmas, two guests in our house
Were playing some bridge against me and my spouse.
Please tell me, she shouted "Why didn't you double?
Twas plain from the start that we had them in trouble."

"Tis futile, my Dear—I am taking no stand
So please stop your nagging. Let's play the next hand."
"Remember next time," she said with a frown,
"To double a contract that's sure to go down."

So I picked up my cards in a downtrodden state,
Then I opened one spade and awaited my fate:

Dealer East, N-S vulnerable

North
♠ 9876
♡ 65432
◇ 8765
♣ —

West		East (Me)
♠ —	┌─────────┐	♠ AKQJ10
♡ QJ109	│ 2♠ DBL │	♡ AK87
◇ KQJ109	│♡Q LEAD │	◇ —
♣ KQJ10	└─────────┘	♣ A987

South
♠ 5432
♡ —
◇ A432
♣ 65432

The guy sitting South was like many I've known.
He bid and he played in a world all his own.
"Two diamonds," he countered with scarcely a care:
The ace in his hand gave him courage to spare

My wife, smiling faintly and tossing her head,
Leaned over the table: "Double!" she said.
And North for some reason I cannot determine
Bid two hearts like she was preaching a sermon.

I grinned as I doubled enjoying the fun,
And turned 'round to South to see where he'd run.
But South, undistressed nor at loss for a word
Came forth with "Two spades"—Did I hear what I heard?

The other two passed and in sheer disbelief
I said, "Double, my friend, that'll bring you to grief!"
South passed with a nod, his composure serene,
My wife with a flourish led out the heart queen.

I sat there and chuckled inside o'er their fix,
But South very calmly ran off his eight tricks.
He ruffed the first heart in his hand right away,
And then trumped a club on the board the next play.

He crossruffed the hand at a breathtaking pace
'Til I was left holding five spades to the ace.
In anguish my wife cried "Your mind's growing old
You should see that six notrump for us is ice-cold!!"

By doubling this time I'd committed a sin—
It just goes to prove that you never can win.

Bridge Jargon

Balancing Double — A takeout double made in balancing seat. Lighter values and imperfect distribution are possible.

Bergen Raises — Convention that allows responder to define his strength and precise number of trumps in support of partner's 1♡ or 1♠ opening.

Crawling Stayman — Variation of Stayman featuring a 2♣ response with a weak hand and length in both majors. After opener's 2◇ rebid, 2♡ by responder signifies "crawling." Opener now chooses a major.

DONT — **D**isturbing **O**pponent's **N**o**T**rump, a.k.a. Bergen Over Notrump. Emphasizes distribution, not points. With a two-suited hand, overcall in your lower-ranking suit. Double with a one-suited hand. Bid 2♠ with spades.

Drury — A 2♣ response to a third- or fourth-seat opening of 1♡ or 1♠ promises support for the major and a maximum passed hand.

Fourth-Suit Forcing to Game — Artificial bid of the fourth (unbid) suit that commits the partnership to at least a game contract.

Garbage Stayman — Stayman bid with a weak hand short in clubs. Responder usually intends to pass opener's rebid.

Jacoby Transfer — Used in response to notrump opening bids, or a natural notrump overcall. A diamond bid promises heart length, while a heart response shows at least five spades. Opener must bid the suit responder has "shown." One of the most important modern conventions.

Jacoby 2NT — Artificial game-forcing raise of opener's major suit. Opener's first responsibility is to show a singleton.

Jordan 2NT — After a double of partner's opening bid in a suit, a jump to 2NT promises ten or more points with four trumps.

LAW of Total Tricks — aka.The LAW. Helpful to all players when judging whether to bid on in competitive auctions. Based on the concepts that "trump length is everything." Discovered by Jean René Vernes, expanded by Marty Bergen, and popularized in Larry Cohen's classic book, *To Bid or Not to Bid.*

Lead-Directing Double — Double of an artificial bid, promising length and strength in suit named. Some examples are doubles of *Stayman, Jacoby Transfers*, and responses to *Blackwood.*

Michaels Cuebid — An overcall in the opponent's suit that shows at least five cards in two other suits. The emphasis is on the unbid major(s).

Negative Double — Responder's double after partner opens the bidding and RHO makes a natural overcall. It promises some values and emphasizes the unbid major(s). Absolutely essential for winning bridge.

1NT Forcing — Convention in which a 1NT response to partner's major-suit opening in first or second position cannot be passed. This is often used with *two-over-one game forcing.* Popular among duplicate players.

1NT Semi-Forcing — Bergen variation of 1NT Forcing. Opener is allowed to pass with a balanced minimum.

"Points Schmoints" — A Bergenism that emphasizes trumps and shape, while de-emphasizing HCP.

Prime Cards — Aces and kings, as opposed to queens and jacks.

Proven Cards — Honor cards that are expected to be helpful to partner. Aces and kings are proven, as are honors in partner's suit(s).

Puppet Stayman — After a 1NT opening, a jump to 3♣ response asks opener if he holds a four- or five-card major.

Reverse — Opener's rebid at the two level in a higher-ranking suit than his first bid shows at least 17 points and promises five or six cards in his first suit. This topic causes more anxiety than any other.

Reverse Drury — Variation of Drury in which opener signs off in the agreed major at the two level if he has no interest in game.

Roman Keycard Blackwood — Popular modern convention where the trump king is treated as the "fifth" ace. The trump queen is also referenced.

Rule of 11 — Applied to fourth-best leads. The numerical value of the card led is subtracted from 11; the difference represents the number of higher cards held by the other three players.

Rule of 20 — Used to evaluate whether to open borderline hands in first and second seat. Add the length of your two longest suits to your HCP. With 20 or more, open the bidding in a suit at the one level.

Sacrifice — A bid made with no expectation of making the contract. The player hopes to lose fewer points than the opponents would have scored if allowed to play in their contract.

Smolen — After responder bids Stayman and opener bids 2◊, responder's bid of three of either major promises five cards in the unbid major.

Snapdragon — A double by fourth hand after the other three players have each bid their own suit.

Splinter Raise — Conventional jump into a short suit (0 or 1 card), promising good support for partner and values for game or slam.

Texas Transfer — Jump to 4◊ or 4♡ in response to an opening notrump bid. Responder has the suit above the one he bids.

2♣ Opening — A strong, artificial and forcing opening bid used with powerhouse hands when playing weak two-bids. Opener either has a long suit, or a balanced hand too strong to open 2NT.

3♣ Second Negative — (aka double negative) After an uncontested auction begins 2♣-2♦ and opener bids two of a major, responder's 3♣ is weak.

Two-Over-One Game Forcing — Convention in which responder's two-level response to an opening bid in a major is forcing to game. Not applicable in competition or by a passed hand.

Two-Way Drury — Bergen variation where responder's 2♦ bid promises a fourth trump. Therefore, the 2♣ response shows exactly three-card support for opener's major.

Two-Way Reverse Drury — Convention that combines Reverse Drury and Two-Way Drury.

Unusual NT Overcall — A method of showing length in the two lower unbid suits after an opponent opens at the one level. If an opponent opens a major, 2NT promises at least five cards in each minor.

Vulnerable, Schmulnerable — Bergenism which suggests that a player should not be afraid to bid just because he is vulnerable.

Weak Jump Raise — An effective tool for preemptively raising partner's bid in a competitive auction. Based on *The Law of Total Tricks*.

Weak Jump Shift in Competition — Recommended treatment in which responder's jump shift shows weakness after an opponent has bid or doubled.

Weak Two-Bid — An opening preempt in diamonds, heart or spades. The bid traditionally promises 5-10 HCP and a strong six-card suit.

Index

Learning With Marty

If you enjoyed *More Points Schmoints!* you might want to consider ordering one or more of the following publications.(Ordering details can be found on page 210.) Bridge books make a thoughtful gift for your card-playing friends and family, too. Thank you, and happy reading!

By Marty Bergen

More POINTS SCHMOINTS!   Hardcover — $19.95

POINTS SCHMOINTS! (1996 Book of the Year) Hardcover — $19.95

* * Special: Order both POINTS SCHMOINTS books for $35 * *

Better Bidding With Bergen Volume 1
   — Uncontested Auctions $11.95

Better Bidding With Bergen Volume 2
   — Competitive Bidding $9.95

Everyone's Guide to the New Convention Card   SALE ~~$9.95~~ $7.95

By Larry Cohen

To Bid or Not to Bid — The Law of Total Tricks $12.95

Following the Law — The Total Tricks Sequel $12.95

All books by Marty and Larry will be sent with personalized autographs upon request. A free gift from Marty will accompany every order.

*   *   *

Highly Recommended

Please visit Marty at **The Bridge Forum International School**. I will be providing bridge tips and articles, as well as answering questions. You can find us at: http://www.bridge-forum.com.

Future bridge cruises with Marty. If interested, call 800/367-9980.

By Burt Hall and Lynn Rose-Hall

    How the Experts Win at Bridge $16.95

By Edwin B. Kantar

    A Treasury of Bridge Tips $10.95
    Take Your Tricks (Declarer) $11.95
    Eddie Kantar Teaches Modern Bridge Defense $19.95
    Eddie Kantar Teaches Advanced Bridge Defense $19.95

By Michael Lawrence

    Disturbing Opponents' No Trump (45 pages) $5

*   *   *

Bridge Calendars Year 2000 *(Marty's week of Q & A begins August 5)*
    365 interesting bridge deals with expert analysis   SALE $12
    * * Special - Year 1999 $5

DEALMASTER Software
    Generates deals for teaching and playing   SALE $54

*   *   *

To place your order, please send a check or money order (U.S. dollars) to:

Marty Bergen
9 River Chase Terrace
Palm Beach Gardens, FL 33418-6817
Credit card orders are also welcome.
1-800-386-7432
E-mail: mbergen@mindspring.com

Please include $3 postage and handling.
***Postage is free* if your order includes:**
More POINTS SCHMOINTS!* or *POINTS SCHMOINTS!
Florida state residents please add 6% sales tax